CW00519229

FINDING

THE LOST CITY OF

ATLANTIS

BY

DR MORVEN ROBERTSON

The Author

Dr Morven Robertson was born in 1954. Awarded the Elgin scholarship by Bedford School, Exhibition to Queens' College, Cambridge University qualified with MA and PhD (Cantab). Worked first in R&D on missile systems and subsequently other leading high technology companies and is currently CEO and director life-science and high tech companies. He has published papers in learned journals on scientific discoveries including the invention of a laser interferometer.

He has applied his considerable scientific knowledge with his strengths in finding solutions to complex multi-disciplinary problems to the Atlantis story in the belief that it contained a large amount of truth which lay buried beneath misconceptions. His research in this area is the product of over 20 years of study across a wide range of disciplines. It has become solvable with recent advances in technology and research that have provided unparalleled access to vast amounts of information hitherto unobtainable.

First published in Great Britain 2014

Copyright © 2014 by Morven Robertson

All rights reserved. This publication cannot be reproduced, stored in a retrieval system, or transmitted by any means without the prior permission in writing of the publisher, nor be otherwise circulated in any form of binding or cover other than which it is published and without a similar condition including this condition being imposed on the subsequent purchaser. Author does not own the copyright to any of the illustrations.

Author Morven Robertson

About Atlantis   Finding the Lost City of Atlantis

Published by About Atlantis Ltd

Milton Keynes, England

October 2015

CONTENTS

List of Illustrations

32. Mud volcano in Apennine mountains south of Po plain
33. Photo of the moment a tsunami hits coast in Japan
34. Map of earthquake storm in Po valley
35. Aftereffects of an avulsion of the Saskatchewan river in Alaska
36. Map of Urnfield culture in Europe
37. Photo of Bristlecone pine tree in Yosemite
38. Halley's comet as depicted in Bayeaux tapestry
39. Photo of recent asteroid in sky over Russia just before impact
40. Photo of destruction caused by meteorite in Siberia in 1908
41. Map of distribution of Y-DNA R1b chromosome in Europe
42. Map of R-S28 subgroup linked to Urnfield groups
43. Map of bell beaker sites in Europe
44. Sample of chalcopyrite copper ore
45. Phoenecian coin showing two pillars of Heracles
46. The Nebra diskA
47. Gold Conus hats found in south Germany
48. Gold Lunulae found in United Kingdom
49. The Trondheim chariot from Denmark
50. A bronze cauldron from the Villanovian culture of north Italy
51. Aerial photo of Amsterdam showing the canals in circular rings
52. Example of beaker which gives name to the bell-beaker culture
53. Bronze idol with horns from Cyprus possibly Baal
54. Effigy of a Bull's head used for religious practices from Knossos
55. The horns of consecration at Knossos
56. Inscribed gold plates of court records from Persepolis
57. Clay tablet with Linear A text from Minoan Crete
58. Tablet with Linear B text from Mycenaean Crete
59. Schematic of Inka knot method of record keeping
60. Pair of Bronze Age Lurs from Denmark
61. Round shield from Scotland
62. The Waterloo helmet from Bronze Age, found by Thames
63. Bronze Age weapons found in Romania
64. Aerial view of Stonehenge

98. Photo of Salzburg showing Danube and Castle
99. Salzburg castle
100. St Michael's Mount in Cornwall, UK
101. Mont St Michel in Brittany, France
102. The River Elbe flowing through southern Germany
103. The Ringen Roysa from Avaidsnes in Norway
104. The citadel at Budapest
105. Amber washed up on Danish coast
106. Statue of Zeus
107. Erecthion on the Acropolis at Athens
108. Ruins at Tiryns
109. Bull leapers painting at Knossos
110. Pottery picture of Theseus slaying the Minotaur
111. Statue of Atlas holding world on his shoulders
112. Statue of the god Resheph from Gebal
113. Wall painting at Akrotiri in Santorini
114. The Dupljaja chariot
115. The Uffington white horse
116. Replica of the Jason's boat the Argo
117. The Dikteon cave in Crete
118. The Egyptian goddess Neith
119. Hellenistic period statue of Icarus
120. Strettweg Chariot from Urnfield Culture
121. Abbots Bromley horn dance
122. Raising the Maypole in Bas Rechenhall
123. Pottery painting of Odysseus blinding the Cyclopes
124. Egyptian Empire in 15 century BC
125. Map of possible route of the Argo
126. Statue of Poseidon as human stereotype
127. Minoan snake goddess from Knossos
128. Excavations at Sais
129. Map of Sais by J.Champollion
130. Gold cup from Mycenae

131. Sanctuary of Apollo at Delphi, Greece
132. Scandanavian Bronze Age rock carvings
133. Megalithic stone ship at Badekunda
134. Cronus hat calendar chart
135. Egyptian tablet showing snake gods
136. Stone from Coldfield, UK
137. Adige valley in Italy
138. Nuraghe village in Sardinia
139. Bronze-age settlement in Sicily
140. Monkodonja site near Rovigo in Istria
141. Taula stone pillar in Majorca
142. Los Millares Bronze Age site in southern Spain
143. Bronze Age fort at Veronella near Verona,Italy
144. House in Skara Brae, Orkneys

Preface

The legend of Atlantis has long fascinated people from all walks of life and has been the subject of numerous books and theories as to its location. Much of what is known has been discussed in these various works, but very recent advances in technology and so in knowledge have now made it possible to re-examine the story to determine whether or not it is a factual account and if so where the location is on the basis of this new information.

I have spent many years looking into the claims made in this story on a part time basis and have acquired sufficient knowledge to be able to get behind the story to the real facts contained within the accounts given by Plato nearly two and a half thousand years ago and now as a result of new information am able to write this book and understand the sequence of events and identify the actual location of the city and plain referred to in the Atlantis dialogue.

This story is particularly relevant to our time. Topically, it recalls how climate change caused civilisation to collapse throughout the western world and of how society at the time was unable to deal with the consequences. It led to a dark age in which most of the records and memories of previous times became lost or reinvented as myths.

The Atlantis story is particularly important to our history, because it tells us much about a time of which we have no written records, of how a large and well organised society flourished in these regions before 1000bc and that, after calamities that spanned Europe and the Mediterranean late in that millennium, the history of their achievements as well as those of the Greeks were lost but by luck a recollection had been saved in records kept by Egyptian monks at Sais, this survived into Classical times and these were subsequently written down and transcribed by Plato in his works.

Chapter 1

The story behind Atlantis

Well, the good news is that you can actually visit the lost island of Atlantis. It is here in Europe and you can also see the last remnant of the capital city of a lost kingdom that once held sway over much of Europe, the Rock of Monselice in the Po valley. It was once the ancient acropolis of this kingdom and can be seen today, just as you see it in the photograph on the front cover.

When you hear Atlantis mentioned you probably imagine an island in ancient times suddenly subject to earthquakes and horrendous geological events that sank under the sea, wiping out all its inhabitants in a catastrophic event.

So where did this story come from. It is well known that the written source of this legend originates in a work by the philosopher Plato. Plato lived in Athens in ancient Greece in the 4th century BC and was a student of Socrates, the famous philosopher. Plato spent much of his time studying, lecturing and writing on matters such as the nature of society, the origins of the universe and the world we live in. He was a highly regarded intellectual in his own day.

The story of Atlantis appears in his books Timaeus and Critias and according to Plato was a true recital of a story passed down to him through his ancestors from Solon, an Athenian statesman of great stature. Solon had made a visit to Egypt where it is claimed he had been told the story by Priests in Sais (a town on the Nile delta) who had kept extensive written records of major events across the known world stretching far back into antiquity. Plato claims he wanted to use the story in a discussion concerning the nature of society in his work Timaeus as an example of a type of society that was relevant to the discussion because it was a real example of a highly organised ancient society in his opinion and so had merit in the discussions taking place in his book. The account of Atlantis appears in brief in Timaeus, but Critias, the second work, is specifically devoted to the story of both ancient Athens and Atlantis and goes into great detail about Atlantis.

The two dialogues that concern the myth of Atlantis, the short one in Timaeus and the lengthier one in Critias are attached as transcripts in an Appendix at the end of this book.

Plato states that the story of was passed down to him by a relation, his mother's cousin, a man named Critias who had received it from his great grandfather, called Dropides who was a relation and friend of the Solon who was a leading figure and famous lawmaker in Athens. Solon had travelled extensively throughout the Mediterranean and had visited Sais in Egypt, the capital during this Saite dynastic period. He had received the story from priests when he visited Sais which was located near Alexandria in the Nile delta and had translated it from Egyptian and written it down in Greek. Plato explains

that when he was ten years old and his grandfather nearly ninety, that he remembers the story being recited at a festival for children, held annually in Greece, called Apatouria by a poet, Amynander, who was a clansman or family member related to Critias. He also claims he had read and studied the manuscript extensively when a child.

The next question is did Plato actually believe the story to be true. Plato is regarded as being one of the greatest philosophers of all time. He analysed

Figure 1   A Roman artists idea of Plato's academy from a mosaic uncovered in the ruins of Pompeii dated to first century AD

very complex subject matters and would look to examples from the real world to use in his arguments in order to assist in the analyse of matters such as the nature of existence in assessing alternative systems of government and in the case of political systems in the belief that a better model could be developed with the aim of leading to a advancement in the functioning of society.

Plato was born around 428bc a few years after the Parthenon had been completed in Athens at the height of Athens as a power. At the time Plato was living, philosophy was a relatively new subject and had until very recently been basically esoteric, however in this new and prosperous society with its more liberal attitudes, leading thinkers of the time such as Socrates had begun to move from simply an academic approach into looking into and questioning society directly and so had come into conflict with both the establishment of the time in Athens and also its religious leaders. Socrates was charged with corrupting the minds of the youths and with impiety (not believing in the state gods). We owe Solon and many others living at these times a huge debt for their contribution to the advancement of society. Socrates upset the establishment and paid the price with his life, we can assume this left a lasting impression on his student Plato, so Plato's arguments were not trivial matters.

So would Plato have fabricated a story, which he claimed was real, to make a point in a discussion about an important subject. I believe it would have been pointless and the only reason Plato used it was that he believed it had value as it was true. The counter argument that he invented it for the purposes of proving a point is also undermined by the large amount of unnecessary detail in the dialog in Critias.

Figure 2 The Acropolis in Athens. The Parthenon was competed in 432bc around Plato's birth

This of course does not mean that Critias could not have invented it, or Solon, or even the priests that told it to Solon. In fact if anyone had fabricated the story it could have been the priests, as Solon had only their word for its truth and they may have wished to please him.

Solon was a great statesman and likewise was unlikely, in my view, to have made it up and has he lived at the same time as Plato's ancestor it also seems unlikely that the story could have been attributed to Solon without his agreement, so we are left with the priests at Sais.

They could have made the story up to please Solon but the detail seems to be far beyond what was required if they simply wanted to pander to Solon by telling him of the great achievement of

Figure 3 Map of Nile delta in the Bronze Age

his city in former terms. If anything, it is this claim rather than the detail about the respective societies in ancient Attica (where Athens is located in Greece) and Atlantis that may have been embellished.

Plato again says in Critias that he had a manuscript that he studied extensively as a child. This adds to the argument that certainly that Solon had brought back the story after visiting Egypt.

Plato mentions hearing the speech at the festival of Apatouria. This was a festival where children were introduced into a Phatry, similar to a Clan or Fraternity, to which they would become full members in adulthood. This festival involved the children partaking in both games and intellectual activities, such as poetry recitals. It was a celebration of the groups from which Athens had come together in ancient times and hence this dialogue would have been appropriate as an entry for the poetry competition. The next question to look into to establish the truth of this story is does the chronology of how the story was passed down fit with the timescales of the lives of the participants. We know Plato lived from 428 to 348bc and Solon from 638 to 558bc. Even with small errors in these dates the chronology would fit with what we are told, allowing for typical ranges in our lifespans and how the story passed down through the generations described.

So if we accept that the story was essentially conveyed as true by all parties, where would the island called Atlantis have been located and what happened to it. To understand the facts of the story one must read the text in great detail before coming to any conclusions. We should check the statements being made and see if they fit with what we know about this period. **I will refer to the texts of Timaeus and Critias as the dialogue to distinguish them in future from other texts being referred to.**

The very first point is that Plato at no point in his dialog says the island completely disappeared below the sea. He refers to Atlantis in the dialogue as 'it sank below the sea' and also as 'shoal mud being where the island had stood' and he does not state that everyone died as a result. Also, he is unclear as to whether the island he referred to was simply the main part of an island or the whole area around it. Also, the dialog does not tell us where this sea was.

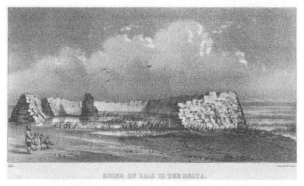

Figure 4   The remains of the Temple of Neith dated 1855 by Lowth entitled Ruins of Sais in the Delta. Nothing of this temple remains above ground today. Farmers removed the bricks for use in local constructions.

The dialogue starts with Solon telling some of the mythical stories of the Greeks and being interrupted by an elder priest who says 'Oh Solon, Solon you Greeks are but children, there's no such thing as an ancient Greek and after giving examples how the myths   were interpretations of actual historical events   and goes on to say 'the genealogy of your own people which you were just recounting is little more than children's stories'. In other words that the stories of the gods that the Greeks were familiar with were about real people and events but without historical reference and simplified for general consumption and for religious purposes.

While Plato recorded the story to illustrate a point in his argument he may well have also had a second motive when he points out that the Sais priests referred to the myths of the Greeks as being only children's stories. He was entering dangerous ground when pointing out that the religious stories about Zeus and other Greek gods could be based around real events and distorted for religious reasons and that the stories that formed the basis for the Greek religion were actually about real people and not Gods or otherworldly beings.

Both the start and finish of his dialog touch on issues concerning Greek religious beliefs, this was not accidental and finishes the way it does for precise reasons, yet this in no way invalidates the story of Atlantis contained within the dialog.

In Timaeus, the priests explain to Solon that the Greek remembrance of the flood of Deucalion, a mythical flood that occurred in ancient times, and also that of Phaeton (according to legend he stole the chariot of the sun from his father Helios but could not steer it and crashed into the sea) were based on real climatic and meteorological events. The priests pointed out both that floods had occurred periodically in many regions throughout history and that comets and meteorites were also frequent occurrences and sometimes have either just missed, or on occasions have even hit, the earth.

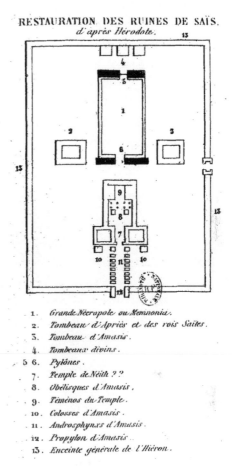

RESTAURATION DES RUINES DE SAÏS.
d'après Hérodote.

1. Grande Nécropole ou Memnonia.
2. Tombeau d'Apriès et des rois Saïtes.
3. Tombeau d'Amasis.
4. Tombeaux divins.
5 6. Pylônes.
7. Temple de Néith ??
8. Obélisques d'Amasis.
9. Téménos du Temple.
10. Colosses d'Amasis.
11. Androsphynxs d'Amasis.
12. Propylon d'Amasis.
13. Enceinte générale de l'Hiéron.

Figure 5 A reconstruction of the layout of the temple at Sais by Francois Champollion

In the case of floods, almost every ancient society has a flood myth, in the bible there is Noah, in Mesopotamia the Summerian's had Ziusudra (their Noah) and the two legends are almost identical, the Greeks Deucalion and the Egyptians were flooded so often that they probably didn't need a myth and as they pointed out to Solon there had not been one flood but numerous throughout their known world since the beginning of time.

17

They go on to say that the greatest achievement of the Athenians had been forgotten, when they had stood up against a great power and defeated it and in so doing had saved both themselves and Egypt from defeat and possibly captivity. They explained the reason for the loss of the memory of this event as being due to a serious of great disasters in which due to hardship and more pressing needs, the number of learned members left to record such events had reduced to such an extent that much of the true history had been lost or replaced with greatly simplified children's stories as basic survival took over from intellectual activities, such as writing and recording of history.

In the dialogue the priests give the time of this war between the Atlanteans and the Greeks, or those that lived within the pillars of Heracles and those outside as having taken place 9000 years before their time. They also referred to the war as that between the followers of Athena and those of Poseidon.

The occupants of the delta at Sais at the time of Solon contained a large number of settlers from the late bronze-age, who also worshipped the goddess Athena (whom they called Neith), like the Athenian's, and who had a lot in common with the Greeks. Athena had originally been a mother goddess figure but, as the cult of Zeus had risen, had been placed below him in the pantheon.

Figure 6   The frieze on the west side of the Parthenon depicted the war between Athena and Poseidon with Athena victorious

Athena was a warrior goddess but in later times was depicted as leaping from the head of Zeus in full armour, showing her place in the Indo European male run society that now dominated the Mediterranean. While Zeus was the Sun God she was, among various accolades, Goddess of the Moon. According to myth, she died and was reborn 12 times a year, as one would expect.

In Plato's dialogue the priests in Sais tell Solon that their sacred records are 8000 years old but that the events described in their records on the pillars were 9000 years old. This seems beyond belief as clearly we know that human society did not evolve into cities such as those described until roughly 3000bc. However the reason for these large numbers of years is that the priests being worshippers of Athena recorded years in terms of her death and rebirth, hence the reference in the dialog to 'sacred records' rather than just records. The cycle of the moon we observe is 29 days and so does not divide exactly into the 365 days of the year. The priests dealt with this by making Athena die and be reborn 12 times a year

Figure 7 The Antikythera mechanism found in the Aegean dates from around 200bc and links solar and the synodic lunar cycles used in Greek religious ceremonies.

and periodically added an extra month to make up the difference. So the 9000

Figure 8 There are around 56 planetary gears making it the most complex mechanism discovered until at least another 1000 years

years mentioned in the dialog translates to 750 years and 8000 to around 670 years. The use of a lunar calendar is corroborated by ancient historians such as Eudoxus of Cnidos and Plutarch, who stated that the Egyptians reckoned their months as a year. The years they give are clearly rounded up approximations, so in reality 8000 should be 8000 years plus or minus 500 years and 9000 also plus-minus 500 lunar years, giving a margin of error of around 40 solar years.

The Athenians used a lunar calendar particularly in liturgical ceremonies. Lunar calendars are extremely old and we now know that the oldest of these calendars date back to the Megalithic period (c.2000- 3000bc). The Egyptians were the first to divide the year into 12 months of 30 days but this meant that after a few years the seasons would start to move out of synchronism with the calendar, to rectify this they introduced extra days periodically, later they introduced an extra month every few years to bring the calendar back into line. Hence, the Antikythera mechanism converted solar and synodic lunar years.

Essentially there were 12 lunar months per calendar year. The monks at Sais would have used 12 lunar months per calendar year in their records. The moon actually takes about 27.5 days to circle the earth but because the earth is also moving around the Sun the actual time between the new moon to full moon and back again, known as the Synodic month is 29.5 days and 12 synodic months equates to about 355 days. This is short by 10 days a year and so every few years has to be adjusted (even if they did not base the calculations on adjusted years the discrepancy over 750 years it would add up to 20 years – so is smaller than the other errors we are considering).

Solon lived from 638bc to 558bc. He was appointed a magistrate in Athens in 594 and after completing reforms he travelled for 10 years during which time he visited Egypt. So we can estimate that the story was told to Solon around 590bc. This places the war

Figure 9 The temple of Medinet Habu where Rameses III is shown defeating the Sea Peoples in carvings on the walls

between the Athenians and the Atlanteans at around 1350bc (plus or minus 40years) and the establishment of the religious community at the delta at around 1250bc (plus or minus 40 years).

The priests at Sais told Solon that they had written records of all major historical events which were preserved in their temples and that this set them apart from the Greeks who has lost or failed to keep record historical events and so had lost all accurate knowledge of them. As mentioned before, this was due to the fact that after the events described a series of calamities overtook the Greeks and that as survival became their main issue and also as many educated people perished, record keeping fell into abeyance and history passed down verbally got distorted. We know that the statement about the records in Egypt bears some truth as the temples in Egypt do hold extensive records painted or carved into them and also written onto papyrus.

Figure 10   Ramases III defeating sea peoples in sea battle on walls at Medinet Habu. The combatants include the Sharda, Lukha,

We do not know how long the war went on for but it ended with victory for the Greek forces according to the dialogue. As Plato says in the dialogue the achievements of these ancient Greeks were not recorded by them and records Solon's surprise when he is told of them. The war could have continued right up to the Trojan War (c.1250bc Troy VI). A short time after this, around 1180 to 1200bc, severe earthquakes and climatic disasters seem to have significantly contributed to the collapse of civilisations in the Aegean and Anatolia, however Athens countered the general decline and it does appear that it survived during this period partly due to the strength of its defences.

Records show that vast numbers of displaced peoples were travelling around the Mediterranean from around 1250bc to 1150bc. Inscriptions made by Ramses II record his victory over the so called Sea Peoples and note their desperate condition. The Sea Peoples were a group of sea borne marauders who patrolled the coasts of the Eastern Mediterranean and initially raided towns for provisions but later tries to occupy lands at various places.

We nowCrete was home to the Minoan civilisation that thrived during the second millennium. They controlled the seas in the Eastern part of the

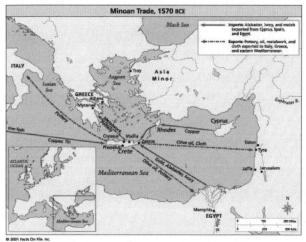

Mediterranean and kept pirates at bay. However, Crete was hit by Tsunamis after a volcanic eruption at Santorini (Thera) at a time which is the subject of some debate but currently placed at around 1450bc and which had a devastating effect on it. This event was devastating

Figure 11 Minoan trade at around 1570bc at height of its power

for the Minoan civilisation and its dominance of trade in the eastern Mediterranean which subsequently began a decline. There is evidence of another disaster around or just after 1450bc which appeared to be an invasion, Knossos palace was rebuilt about 1400bc and then at roughly 1375bc the destruction of the palaces and the end of the Minoan civilisation occurred, which was followed by the Mycenaean occupation of Crete. The power vacuum created by the eruption in 1450bc probably led to a period of lawlessness in the western Mediterranean. The reality of the Mycenaean civilisation as it is called is far more likely to have been a confederation of city

states with varying systems of government and laws which acted together in times of mutual crisis through an alliance but otherwise competed with each other. We know from archaeological evidence that the civilisation of the Minoans came to an end just before the rise of Mycenae and that after the Santorini eruption. Excavations show that Minoan Crete was sacked and burned before 1350bc by as yet unidentified peoples prior to it

Figure 12 The extent of Mycenaean Empire from 1400 to 1100bc

being taken over by the Mycenaeans at about this time.

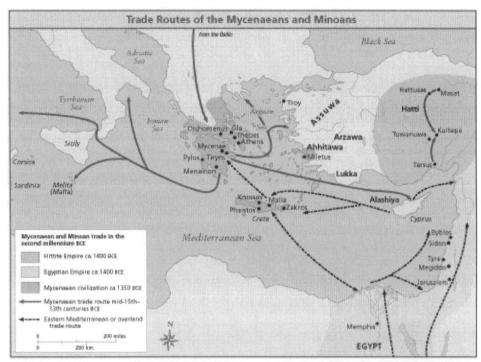

Figure 13 Mycenaean trade routes. Trade did not extend as far as the Atlantic or into the Black Sea.

The Phaestos disk (dated at 2nd millennium, possibly 14th century) shows characters inscribed which closely resemble the images of the sea peoples inscribed in stone on buildings in Egypt. These sea peoples have been variously identified as being Atlanteans, Trojans, Dorians, Sardinians, Thracians, Greeks and many other. So the power vacuum described above that existed at the time of the war in the dialogue led to the Atlantis expansionism referred to.

We next need to look at the location of the island of Atlantis to see if there is an obvious place that fits with the description in the dialogues and would be relevant in archaeological and historical terms.

The description of the plain of Atlantis describes and area around roughly 200x300 miles in size, (the dialog gives the dimensions as 3000x2000 stadia and one stadium is around 600ft). The dialog states that the island of Atlantis sank under the sea and that shoal mud is now there. We now have plans of the ocean floor around the world and such a large area should be easy to locate. There are a number of possible locations. However, it is important to remember that while at the time of the story, Atlantis had disappeared under

23

the sea, that does not mean that today it could now be dry land or a simply a sand or mud bank. There is one very important clue. The plain was surrounded by large mountains on three sides higher than those that exist today. This statement 'exist today' may be an example of an assumption that is an error by the author of the dialog or that they are not known at this time as they lay out of the sphere of knowledge of authors of the dialog through being unreachable or otherwise. As we know there are no such mountains buried under the ocean due to historically recent subsidence and that they could not have simply disappeared. At one time the North Atlantic Ridge was proposed, however we are talking in terms of millions rather than thousands of years, so this is not a candidate.

Figure 14 The current boundary marker in Gibralter claiming to be site of ancient pillars of Heracles

What we can safely assume is that a power sufficient to challenge all the other powers that existed in the Mediterranean at the time and that had the resources described would had to have occupied a large area and have a large number of inhabitants, this would rule out all small islands and the like. We can also safely assume that archaeological records of these people exist but her have not been found or not identified with them.

The dialogue refers to a power beyond 'the pillars of Heracles' and also refers to the furthest part of the island as opposite Gadeira, which was given to Eumulus one of the sons of Poseidon and the twin of Atlas who was first king of Atlantis according to the dialog. The straits can be assumed as Gibralter and Gadeira still exists today as Cadiz, on this there seems to be general agreement. The pillars of Heracles at the time that Plato was writing would have referred to those of Gibralter, although, in antiquity, there were many pillars of Heracles referred to at numerous locations throughout the Mediterranean. The most likely theory is that these pillars served as territorial or boundary markers and were set up to let travellers know whose waters they were now entering. There are pillars today in such places as the entrance to St Mark's Square in Venice. The followers of Heracles were known as the Heracleides and it seems likely they raised the pillars in various places within the Mediterranean. However, the reference to these pillars became attached to those at the straits of Gibralter in later Greek writings and almost certainly by the time of Solon.

They governed their own territories and many islands in the Ocean according to the dialog, which would logically seem to refer to the Atlantic region. 'Inside the Mediterranean' the text states 'they controlled populations as far as Tyrrhenia (North-west Italy) and up to the borders of Egypt (Libya)'. It also refers to a confederacy of kings ruled over by the king of the main island. It is clear from the dialog that a large area is being discussed for the whole island as opposed to the region around the capital city. Hence the comment about it being bigger than Libya and Asia combined.

Figure 15 World map according to Homer

One of the problems in understanding writings of this time is that while the Greeks and Egyptians had a reasonable understanding of the geography of the Mediterranean, they had virtually no knowledge of what lay beyond, either in the Atlantic Ocean or in the Adriatic other than close to its mouth, south of modern day Albania. Even the Romans in the first century AD had virtually no knowledge of the boundaries of present day Germany or of Britain. Julius Caesar was under the impression Britain was a huge land and was dismayed when it turned out to be much smaller than he had expected. The Baltic remained a permanent mystery to the Romans.

One also has to be careful with names they allocated to the seas. The Greeks referred to the sea beyond the pillars of Heracles or the Atlantic, as the Ocean and sometimes the Chronian Sea but they referred to the northern part of the

Adriatic specifically as the Chronian Sea. There are a string of islands that run across the south Adriatic and these probably formed a natural boundary between the Mycenaeans and the inhabitants of the northern Adriatic. The term Chronian Sea more likely referred to seas controlled by other peoples. They were familiar with the fact that the Mediterranean is not tidal and that the Atlantic is and there are frequent references to this, hence they understood the difference between a sea and an ocean. This is not surprising as the Atlantic had been navigated from the Mediterranean since early in the third millennium.

The use of the word controlled in the dialog, as opposed to being part of their own territories when referring to Tyrrhenia and Libya, shows that the Atlanteans were a colonial power and excercised control over foreign territories within the Mediterranean putting them under their sphere of influence.

We can safely assume the details of the island of Atlantis given in the dialog were obtained by interrogation of prisoners or by intelligence gained by the Egyptians during the time of Akenhaten. The Egyptians, however, did not venture into the Mediterranean and relied on other parties to move most of the goods around. Their knowledge of the Mediterranean was therefore somewhat sketchy beyond the Eastern end. One

Figure 16 The Pharaoh Akenhaten who lived around the time of the war in the dialog and saw Egypt's influence in external world affairs diminish

reason for this was the extensive numbers of pirates that operated in the western part and also that the Minoans had corned the market in sea trade in the central Mediterranean and were able to keep the pirates in the west at bay. So the description of an island could mean anything from what we call an actual island to a region of the coast or simply an area of land anywhere surrounded mostly by water. Hence the confusing statement that "the island of Atlantis was surrounded by high mountains'. In fact all that you get from the text is that a canal running around the border of the plain around the city defined the area as an island rather than a valley. We know the southern side was open to the sea and that the capital was roughly central to this side and close to the sea as one would expect if it was a major port.

Figure 17 A geographical map for the Po and Venetian plains showing clearly the Alps, Apennines and Dinaric Alps which surround them as well as the overall shape of the plain

There is only one place in my view that fits this description and that is the Po valley and the area around Venice. There have been many other suggestions as to where Atlantis might be located. Many ignore the bulk of the dialog and simply look for a lost island. This in my view is a pointless exercise. As an example, Thera may have sunk under the sea and been destroyed in a volcanic eruption followed by an inundation, but it absolutely does not fit the bill, as it could never have had the resource to threaten to take over the Mediterranean and threaten Egypt and is far too small to fit the description. A location in the America's would seem to fit the bill, but the idea that it could mount a conquest of the Mediterranean and control its northern shore at that distance would be impossible in the late bronze age. There is also no obvious plain surrounded by high mountains of the size mentioned that faces towards the South of the characteristics and size given. We know from geological surveys of the sea floor that no large mountains have disappeared under the sea. The Atlantic ridge has been investigated extensively and did not sink below the surface in the last few thousand years. In fact there is nowhere on earth where large mountains have sunk below the sea. So we can assume that when the text says that after earthquakes the island sank beneath the sea, it refers to the main island and not the surrounding mountains which must still be exactly where they were 3000 years ago. The Guadalajara valley just beyond Cadiz has also been proposed and seems a likely possibility. However there are several problems. It is just simply not big enough and too remote for the scale of the power being referred to. There are no natural hot water springs nearby as mentioned in the dialog. The dialog also refers to it as being the farthest part of the island and refers to the plain

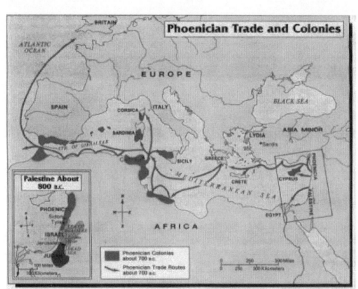

Figure 18 The trade routes and colonies of the Phoenicians around the time of the dialog gives an idea of the known world at that time, the trade up the Adriatic is less that would be expected.

as being close to the centre. It is not surrounded by the highest mountains known of, as the Atlas range are directly opposite and the Sierra Nevada is on the inside of the straits. The Alps fit the description and the only other range would be the Himalayas, but clearly they are in completely the wrong place from the dialogue. Turkey has also been mentioned but again does not fit.

The island of Santorini and the other islands in the Aegean Sea do not fit the description nor does Malta, which has also been proposed, as again it is far too small. Troy fits part of the description but again the plain is far too small and there is no evidence of the other features mentioned in the dialog, particularly its reference to islands in the ocean beyond the pillars of Heracles. Troy is definitely in the Mediterranean and would not have been referred to as outside it and there is no plain of the size mentioned.

This leaves the northern Atlantic seaboard. Again we have the problem with the size of the plain and the mountains. The culture of this area would be very much the same as that in the Po valley and they would have probably been part of the confederation of 10 regions referred to in the dialogue. The size of the domain of Atlantis is referred to as larger than Libya and Asia combined.

So we are talking about a very large land area. This means it can only be either Europe or America that is being referred to.

Figure 19 Mud banks close to Po delta today along with low lying marshland make navigation difficult

In Critias the dialog states that the impenetrable mud prevents free passage of those who sail out of the straits into the open sea. This has been taken to refer to those sailing from Gibralter into the Atlantic or otherwise from the Bosphorus into the black sea. However it could also be referring to those trying to leave the coast of northern Italy trying to sail into the North Sea . In this case the straits being referring to would be the delta of the river Po and access to the Venetian plain.

There is no evidence that a mud bank that halted navigation existed beyond Gibralter along the coast of Portugal existed in the periods we are concerned with.

The other possibility is that the straits refer to the English Channel and that the mud banks are those that do exist along the coasts of Britain and Denmark. It is certainly true that these could have been much more extensive around 1000bc and could have sunk below the sea. They would lie straight ahead from the pillars of Heracles if you sailed along the shoreline. The large mountains could refer to those in Norway, but the general description of any region does not fit that of the text. We are looking for a plain facing south surrounded by large mountains and there is nowhere that fits this description along the coast of Northern Europe. As the Egyptians thought the island existed to the north of the Adriatic and also northwards outside the straits of Gibralter, then mud could have potentially blocked access in both directions from that perspective. Again it is important to remember that they did not have our geographical understanding and that we can assume their map of the world was extremely inaccurate.

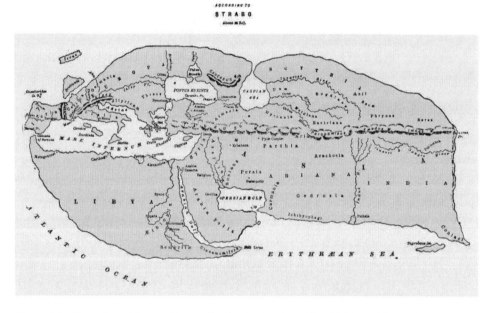

Figure 20 Map of world according to Strabo. Procopius vi/17-23 'the Eridanus has tides but joins the Po shows how they had little concept of the geography of Europe in 1350bc

In the dialog in Critias it gives an outline of the origins of Atlantis in their culture '... when the earth was divided up, Poseidon's share was the island of Atlantis and he settled children borne to him in a particular district of it'. The dialog continues 'At the centre of the island near the sea there was a plain said to be the most beautiful and fertile of all plains and near the middle of the plain about fifty stadia in, a hill of no great size. Here lived one of the original earth born inhabitants called Evenor with his wife Leucippe. They had one child a daughter and Poseidon was attracted to her and had intercourse with her and fortified a hill where she lived by enclosing it with concentric rings of sea and land....' It continues ' ....he begot 5 pairs of male twins, brought them up and divided the island of Atlantis among them...' '....The eldest, the King, he gave a name from which the whole island and surrounding ocean took their designation of Atlantic, deriving it from Atlas their first king. His twin, to whom was allocated the farthest part of the island towards the pillars of Heracles and facing the district now called Gadeira'.

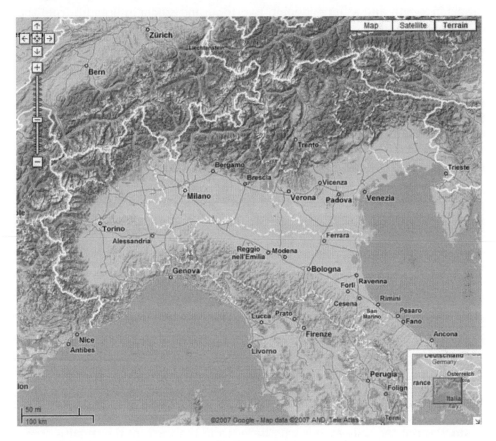

Figure 21 A location for the city somewhere between Padua and Ferrara would fit the location as described at around 1350bc when the coast was further inland than today

The size of the island is given as 3000 stadium as it faces the sea and 2000 stadium in depth (this translates to 300 miles by 200 miles). Being roughly an

31

oblong and where it is not, made more so by canals running around the perimeter. The distance from Trieste to Torino is around 300 miles. The distance northwards from Rimini (the lowest town on the Po valley) to Udine as the crow flies is around 150 miles. However, the distance for taking a sea journey along the coast from Rimini to Trieste would be around 190 miles. It is about the best description for the size of this region you can get without a map and very precise for the time of the dialogue. The town of Este in the Po valley lies almost in the middle of this area being half way both vertically and horizontally and at the time would have been close to the sea. So it accurately fits the description in the dialogue. The dialogue also contains one interested anomaly. It states the island was a rectangle and measured three thousand stadia in length and at its midpoint, two thousand stadia in breadth from the coast. Why not just say its width was 2000 stadia. Two stadia in breadth from the coast is irrelevant if we are simply talking about a rectangle and if not an exact rectangle why not say as later roughly a rectangle. In the Loeb translation we have ' and this plain had a level surface and was as a whole rectangular in shape, 3000 stadia long on either side and 2000 stadia wide at its centre , reckoning upwards from the sea' . It also states in Timaeus that a mighty power was starting from a distant point in the ocean but then later says Atlantis sank beneath the sea and created the mud as it settled down. It places the main island rather than the whole region as close to the sea but the region as bordered by the Ocean.

The writer is trying to convey something else. What is actually being said is that the length along the coast which starts in the middle is 2000 stadia. It is very hard to put into words the shape of the Po and Venetian plains but it is a good description. Rimini is around half way along the length of the plain so the coast starts around here but heads up in a curve towards Trieste. The result is that the plain is not fully rectangular but, as is later said, roughly rectangular with a coast line that starts in the middle and a width that is the same as the distance to follow this coastline..

Plato was not the only author who believed in the truth of the Atlantis story. Aristotle and Strabo both made comparisons between Atlantis and Troy and Posidonious (the Syrian philosopher c90bc) also believed in the Atlantis legend. Interestingly he makes a comment that the dimensions of the Po valley were roughly 3000x2000 stadia and that it was roughly and oblong, he does not go further but clearly it was in his mind.

The dimensions of the Po and Venetian plain fit very closely those described in the dialogue and it is surrounded by the highest mountains in Europe. To the north lie the Alps, with the Apennine mountain chain to the West and the Dinaric Alps to the East, in fact the plain is completely surrounded by mountains and the highest ones in this part of the world as the dialog tells us. In the late Bronze-age it was home to the Terramare culture, where people lived in large villages surrounded by broad canals and extensively farmed cereal and other crops. Their houses were built on stilts and the ditches or canals enclosing them were fed by nearby rivers.

The Terramare culture came to an abrupt end shortly after 1250bc but Villanovian and later Etruscan cultures partly evolved from them.

The problem with this analysis seems to be that the Po valley lies in the Adriatic and not the Atlantic and that the text clearly says a mighty power was advancing from its base in the Atlantic

Figure 22 Reconstruction of a Terramare village at S.Rosa a Fodico di Poviglio near Modena. Houses built on stilts are surrounded by a causeway connecting it to the river

opposite the pillars of Heracles but becomes easier to understand when you realise that they believed the top of the Adriatic was connected directly to the Atlantic. Early maps show the Adriatic heading far to the west in a heavily distorted manner which would have in its extremity made islands out of the Venetian lagoon, Northern Europe and Britain. In Critias is states at the beginning that the it now lies sunk by earthquakes and created a barrier of impassable mud which prevents those who are sailing out from here to the ocean beyond from proceeding further (Loeb pp166) , than later 'Bordering on the sea and extending through the centre of the whole island there was a plain'. He uses sea here rather than ocean. The point I am making from the dialog is that the island faced a sea but gave access to an ocean which had now become inaccessible.

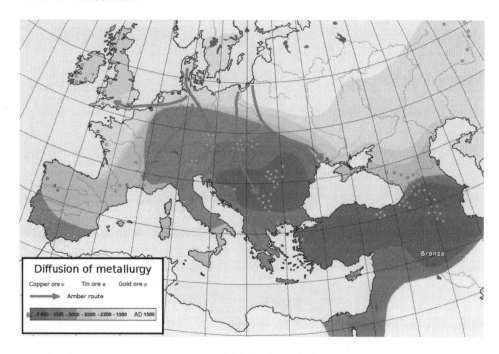

Figure 23 Major sources of Copper during the Bronze-age were located in the Alps and around Salzburg and further west in the Carpathians. The best grade ore came from around the Salzburg area and was transported to the north Adriatic, as it was the closest practical access to the Mediterranean, along with Amber for onward travel by sea as the

Setting aside completely what we know of the geography of the world and imagining what the Egyptians would have understood. They would have probably envisaged the Adriatic as leading to the outer Ocean as did the description of lands beyond the strait of Gibralter. Sea voyages at this time tended to stay close to the shore, so sailing beyond Gadeira would have taken voyagers north and then a long way east as they travelled the northern coat of Spain. It is easy to see how the north of Europe could have become detached according to descriptions and become an island in the Ocean. Likewise the Adriatic would have been assumed be connected to this same sea, as goods such as amber travelled from the Baltic both via Gibralter and via the Adriatic and this would have been mentally assumed as being in the same place as the Po valley by distant countries such as Egypt. The fact that the Po valley lies not towards the South and also was on the wrong side of the Adriatic would not have occurred to them as the description would have made it seem that the city of Atlantis was in the middle of this island beyond Europe in the outer Ocean.

During the late bronze-age there were extensive connections throughout Europe. One particularly important trace route was the amber trade route, which linked the Baltic regions and the North Sea coast including eastern Britain to the Po and Rhone rivers via rivers such as the Elbe, Vistula and Oder. This route even reached as far as Mycenae and also the Black Sea criss-crossing the Hungarian plateau and into the Carpathian Mountains.

The Brenner Pass is the easiest route through the Alps from central Europe into Italy. It is just over 4500 feet and is easily passable. There are no real alternatives to the Brenner pass so this has always been critical to North – South European trade It was open in copper age times and goods from Eastern Europe (mainly the Hungarian Basin and the Carpathian Mountains) moved through the pass as did goods (such as amber) from the North, via the Elbe and Moldau Rivers. Likewise goods flowed northwards through this pass.

Figure 24 Brenner Pass is the lowest of all passes from Germany across the Alps into Italy

Just beyond the Brenner Pass in Germany is the Danube, which flows through Munich and this continues eastwards to connect to the Rhine and southerly to the Rhone. So the European trade system was connected by large rivers throughout Europe. The river connecting the Brenner Pass on the Italian side to the Mediterranean is the Adige. So goods would have passed down the Adige and into the Adriatic. Naturally a large port would be required at the point at which the Adige joined the Adriatic and this is the city we are talking about.

A large settlement exists on the Adige at Montagnana dated from around 1100bc this is quite a distance inland (West) up the Adige. At about 800bc this is replaced by a settlement at Este which is much further East of Montagnana and possibly indicates that from the point of access to the sea this was a better position. If the city of the dialogue had been destroyed in around 1150 to 1200bc it is possible a new one was built to replace it but further upstream as the old city was still buried under mud. The events of this time (drought then climate change) had depleted the population and trade had collapsed, so the new city would have been a small affair compared to the previous one.

The alternatives routes by sea involved long hazardous journeys around the West coast of Europe. The route through the Black Sea involved entering hostile territories of the steppes and would still have taken longer and be more hazardous than the route through the Brenner Pass. This did of course require the co-operation of the city states along the way, but by the time we are talking of, the mutual interest in the trade was sufficient to ensure this.

Figure 25 Amber trade routes operating during the middle and late Bronze-age

The Amber trade routes in the Bronze-age have been studied extensively and follow routes from the Baltic to the Mediterranean and Black Sea as shown in the diagram opposite. The route via the Brenner Pass was one of the most important routes serving the Mediterranean.

The societies behind this trading area were clearly heavily interlinked. They had large villages, often built with surrounding ditches or on an island within a small lake, with thatched dwellings which were often on tilts. Examples include those at Wasserburg in Germany, at Montale in the Po valley along with many other places.

Archaeology of the Somerset levels has shown that large farming communities flourished in the late bronze-age and were linked in this case by paths such as the Sweet Track and with enclosed regular fields. It appears that Wessex bronze age society was fairly well organised with little hamlets centred within cultivated areas of fields and tenements. These paths had been in use long before 3000bc and show the considerable history of agriculture in this region.

We also know from a ship recovered from the Hull estuary that large flat bottomed boats were in frequent use along the North Sea seaboard. In fact in the campaigns by Julius Caesar he records the use of local flat bottomed boats which were better suited to the North Sea than the Roman boats.

If we want to look for a northern confederation of states we need look no further. The question arises then as to which location in this region was called the island of Atlantis in the records of the priests and from the description only the Po and Venetian plains fit that of the dialog.

The Greeks new of the river Po as the Eridanus and this was a name they applied to rivers in the far north in general. In Hesiod we get the Eridanos rich in amber. Phaeton and Heliades (daughters of Helios) were changed into black poplars in the Eridanos and Phaeton according to legend fell into the Eridanos (Apollonius of Rhodes). We also have later references to the islands of amber that lie off the Eridanos (Po). There are further references to the screams of Helios's daughters and the stench from the steams of the Eridanos. It is true there are other places with black poplars and also locations for the Eridanos but with the amber islands and the archaeological evidence it would seem that the north Adriatic would be the most likely location. Hesiod refers to '

Eridanos, rich in Amber' and the 'deep eddying Eridanos'. Phaeton and the Heliades were turned into black poplars near the Eridanos (' a river that does not exist anywhere , but is said to be near the Po'Strabo).

Figure 26 The Po delta today is marked by large intermingled tracts of land and water

The importance of the story of Atlantis is not that an island sank beneath the sea without trace but that in the Bronze Age an advanced civilisation existed within Europe of which we know nothing and just as the priests said to Solon the Greek, we are but children who know nothing of our past history it having been destroyed in the ravages of time. In fact Nennius, the British historian did say that the Romans were but a thin veneer on the culture of the inhabitants of this country. The tragedy is that we have lost all our ancient history, the main reason being that it was orally transmitted and not written down deliberately and so no physical record exists and that as its buildings were almost exclusively made from timber, these too have completely disappeared, all we have left after centuries of ploughing and building are a few traces of the past.

Note : I am using dendochronologically corrected dates. Radiocarbon dates are indicated as such where used

Chapter 2

Disastrous droughts, floods and earthquakes

So, what can we find out about the disaster that befell both the Greeks and the Atlanteans. The dialogue in Timaeus refers to 'at a later time there were earthquakes and floods of extraordinary violence and in a single day all your fighting men were swallowed up by the earth and the island of Atlantis was similarly swallowed up by the sea and vanished, this is why to this day the sea in that area is impassable to navigation, which is hindered by mud below the surface, the remains of the sunken island'. In Critias it adds 'it (Atlantis) was subsequently overwhelmed by earthquakes and is the source of impenetrable

mud which prevents free passage of those who sail out of the straits into the open sea'

The dialogues clearly state that both Greece and Athens were subject to some major disasters sometime after the war described in the texts and that this was why knowledge of the war in

Figure 27 Aftermath of a recent earthquake in the Po valley

the dialogues and the history of events before these disasters had been lost. The scale of these disasters was then considerable and must have been enough to cause the collapse of these societies.

It is universally accepted that around 1200bc a major change occurred which led to the collapse of many civilisations in the ancient world. However, the reasons for this collapse have been the subject of considerable debate.

We know that Mycenae was abandoned just after 1200bc. Many of its houses had collapsed after an earthquake and the reduction in population caused by the Trojan was may have contributed to their inability to recover and also defend themselves from attacks from outside. We know Tiryns was buried under several feet of mud in a flash-flood around 1200bc coincident with an earthquake. A century later the Dorians swept in from the north and occupied a virtually empty country. Greece seems to have remained sparsely populated until around 850bc. Herodotus (the famous Greek historian who lived from 482 to 425bc) records that after the Trojan War Crete was so beset by famine and pestilence that it became virtually uninhabited.

Figure 28 Mycenae citadel in ruins after it was destroyed by earthquakes in antiquity

The dialogue in Critias states that Atlantis was overwhelmed by earthquakes. Anatolia, Greece and Italy all sit close to a subduction zone where tectonic plates are colliding creating earthquakes and so volcanoes are therefore also present. A plot of earthquakes in the last thirty years shows how prevalent they are in these regions. We have not experienced a chain of earthquakes similar to ones that have happened in the past, but from archaeological evidence it seems clear that Troy, Mycenae and many other towns were severely damaged by quakes around 1185bc. Recent theories suggest a severe earthquake in northern Anatolia (near Istanbul) could trigger a chain of quakes going westwards as far as Italy.

We also know the Terramare culture came to an abrupt end around this time and the Po delta seems to have been abandoned. The Hittite empire also collapsed at this time and there were large population movements entering Anatolia from northern regions. Sometime after 1209bc when Suppiluliuma II died the Hittite Empire was destroyed. A clay tablet recovered from Ugarit records an attack of the Sea Peoples (which paradoxically was preserved due to the burning of the building around it) but abandonment rather than destruction seems to have the more common occurrence, in line with the migration theory. In 1160bc the Assyrians who bordered the lands of the Hittites to the south in Mesopotamia found themselves dealing with a new people they called the Mushki, who had overrun Cappadocia from the west. They may have simply filled a vacuum after the collapse of the Hittite empire. There is strong evidence linking them to the Bryges who became the Phrygians (Herodotus states that according to the Macedonians the Bryges changed their names to Phrygians after migrating into Anatolia via the Hellespont). It seems that there were major population movements taking place at this time. The origin of the Bryges has been debated but they

Figure 29 Houses of the type that would have been built by the Terramare peoples

are mentioned in many ancient texts and probably came from eastern or north-eastern Europe (as far as the Baltic) by way of Thrace and this is partly confirmed by recent linguistic analysis.

The common denominator appears to be abandonment, without signs of trauma that would normally be associated with conflict. It would seem that survival rather than conquest was the principle reason for the movements. Local populations might have been compelled to move to seek food without realising that the scale of the problem was so large that it would generally not provide a solution. It seems to have affected most of Europe as far as the steppes (with Britain being slightly less affected) extending as far as South as Anatolia, with parts of Africa bordering the Mediterranean also being affected.

We also know that lake deposits in Switzerland show that acidic gaseous deposits were present at this time which had poisoned the water in the lakes and probably affected the soil. We also know that a long period of drought occurred in many places for maybe as long as 30 years followed sometime later by a colder wetter period, this combination of events when added together could easily account for the collapse in civilisations at this time. We know Troy VII was probably destroyed by an earthquake, also the view of Arthur Evans when he visited it.

The cause of these disasters is unknown but there are a number of possibilities but climate change is thought to be the main cause. The proposed causes of this climate change include theories such as dust from a comet passing very close to the earth introducing debris into the atmosphere and volcanic eruptions producing large amounts of ash and gases.

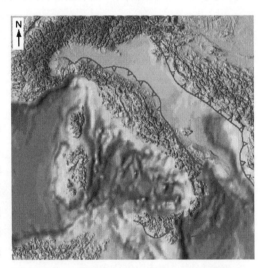

The volcanic eruption of Hekla in Iceland has also been proposed as one cause of the climate change. This pluvian type eruption produces huge amounts of ash and would have actually done much more damage than that at Thera. But we also know that other volcanoes such as Pinatubo erupted close to this time releasing large amounts of sulphur dioxide to the atmosphere

Figure 30 Fault lines where volcanic activity occurs are shown in red extending along Adriatic and far into Po valley along the Apennine chain

that would have caused global cooling. Volcanoes would have emitted loads of fluorine compounds into the atmosphere. These volcanoes could be linked to earthquakes in the Aegean which would have then compounded matters. There are global tree ring records showing a reduction in growth starting at 1159bc which lasted for 18 years and can be linked to Greenland ice sheet records and which may have been caused by reductions in light levels and global cooling. Various scholars have claimed ash from such eruptions could have heavily blocked the sun for up to 3 years and lasted 18 years causing mass starvation.

Ramses II (Pharaoh 1279-1213bc) won a major battle against the sea peoples around 1250bc. Later records show that the Sea Peoples that had invaded the delta were in a bad state and desperately seeking food. This was around 1160bc of Ramses III at a time when we know a long drought had occurred followed by severe floods. He considered them refugees.

It is possible that the dating of Hekla or Pinatubo could vary by several decades and similarly for the dating of the texts from Assyria. If extreme rains caused peoples like the Phrygians to resettle around 1160bc, would assume that the floods had occurred just before that time.

We now need to consider how these events could have affected the northern Adriatic coastal region.

The Po delta and the Venetian lagoon are often subject to severe floods, some up to 3m in depth and also to incursions from the sea. A lot of the Po valley is below sea level and the area like in Venice is constantly sinking. High levels of methane gas are present at the Po delta in thick areas of mud.

The Po valley has a long history of earthquakes and is in a volcanic zone and such features as hot and cold springs are common in volcanic regions. Diffuse degassing can result in gas being dissolved in local groundwater from which springs rise. Such an example occurs in Albani in Italy where there can be sudden releases of gas. The stink referred to as coming from the islands of amber and the Eridanos in numerous texts would fit with this explanation.

Bronze age paleohydrology of the Po and Venetian delta show that the alluvial ridges that were built up by the Po and Adige rivers extended northwards at a maximum during the late Bronze-age by up to 30km from the present positions and that fluvial connection between the Po valley, Venetian plain and Alps was less complex in the early and middle Bronze-age than during the late Bronze-age. Sediments from the rivers in flat plains will build up as alluvial ridges and even today you can see alternate lines of land and water created by deposits around the Po delta.

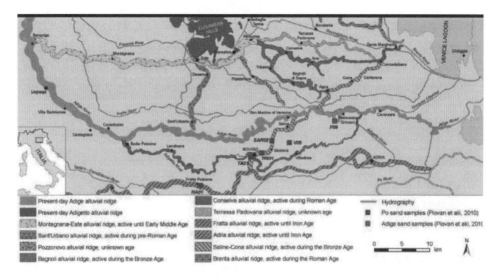

Present-day Adige alluvial ridge
Present-day Adigetto alluvial ridge
Montagnana-Este alluvial ridge, active until Early Middle Age
Sant'Urbano alluvial ridge, active during pre-Roman Age
Pozzonovo alluvial ridge, unknown age
Bagnoli alluvial ridge, active during the Bronze Age

Conselve alluvial ridge, active during Roman Age
Terrassa Padovana alluvial ridge, unknown age
Fratta alluvial ridge, active until Iron Age
Adria alluvial ridge, active until Iron Age
Saline-Cona alluvial ridge, active during the Bronze Age
Brenta alluvial ridge, active during the Roman Age

Hydrography
Po sand samples (Piovan et alii, 2010)
Adige sand samples (Piovan et alii, 2010)

Figure 31 The alluvial ridges created by the Adige and Po rivers are shown from early bronze-age up to present times. The effect of avulsions can be seen when the rivers changed direction in particular the Adige joined the sea in the MBA but after an avulsion in LBA formed its own delta in western Venetian lagoon (Piovan, Siovan)

The whole region has also been sinking at rates of up to 1cm a year but averaging around 2 to 3mm. The Roman town of Altincum was only recently discovered, a matter of 7km north of Venice. It was 2 to 3m above sea level but now has sunk below the surface and only a few walls are visible near to the surface. The current Venetian Grand Canal now appears to have existed at that time and to have run through the centre of the Roman town.

There have been regular severe floods in both the Po and Venetian plains and the worst ones, which have occurred only every few centuries, have seen as much as several feet of water build up. Freak high seas in the Adriatic caused by northerly winds (possibly an effect of El-Nino) could cause flooding and certainly sea has swept in over the land in a similar fashion. There have also been earthquakes the effect of which we know little about. It appears that in the later stages of the Terramare culture the climate worsened and that the water supply was drying up. The canals seem to have emptied and deep wells were dug for water. This fits in with the problems associated with just after 1200bc when a similar experience occurred elsewhere and led to population migration. Like the situation in Mycenae it could well be the case that the drought coupled with a freak event led to the collapse of the community and its abandonment, it is often a combination of calamities that proves the death blow.

The dialogues are slightly confusing regarding the destruction of Atlantis. The dialogue in Timaeus states 'and the island of Atlantis was similarly swallowed up by the sea and vanished, this is why the sea in that area to this day is impassable to navigation, which is hindered by mud just below the surface' and in Critias though it was subsequently overwhelmed by earthquakes and is the source of the impenetrable mud which prevents travel of those who pass out of the straits into the open sea'

The Po valley has been subject to bouts of earthquakes throughout the ages. In November 1570AD a huge earthquake destroyed the city of Ferrara. It was the first of a series of earthquakes that continued for 4 years and levelled most of the area. Bologna had been subjected to an earthquake in 1504AD which was larger than normal and in 1285AD on December 13th an earthquake had

Figure 32 Mud volcano in Apennine mountains just to south of Po valley. These volcanoes emit noxious gases such as hydrogen sulphide producing bad odours over large areas

previously destroyed Ferrara.

The Po valley lies on a subduction zone between tectonic plates. This is caused by compression between the Apennines and Alpine mountains. The Po valley is a sediment filled trough and surprisingly, the Alpide belt is the second most active volcanic belt after the Ring of Fire in Asia.

There are large numbers of mud volcanoes on the south eastern Apennine side of the Po valley. These volcanoes extrude clay, salt water and gases when subjected to earthquakes. There are very large deposits of methane gas in the valley and this is currently being commercial developed by Agip, the Italian state energy company. There are worries that the removal of large amounts of gas could cause serious subduction and studies have raised concerns about this. It is known that after earthquakes, water and gas expulsions have caused large areas of land to settle down and in some cases sea water has rushed in, as happened to a part of Alaska last century.

Figure 33   A tsunami in Japan caused mass devastation as a wall of water rushed inland as captured in the photo above, a subduction caused by an earthquake would have the same effect

The Good Friday Earthquake in Alaska in 1964 caused 70,000 square miles of mostly coastline to subside by 3ft with large areas now flooded by the sea.

The removal of large amounts of ground water might be indicated by the fact that towards the end of the occupation of the delta by the Terramare the wells were becoming increasingly deeper , showing that water was in short supply (probably due to the drought) and that they had to go much deeper to reach the water table. The extraction of large amount of water combined with lowering of the water table would increase the risk of serious subsidence in an earthquake storm as shown in numerous recent studies.

It is also most likely that as natural subsidence had occurred and large amounts of the plain was below sea level that dykes had been constructed to keep the rivers and streams from breaking their banks when water levels were high.

If subsidence occurred, the amount of the delta that would have sunk below sea level would be difficult to estimate. However many

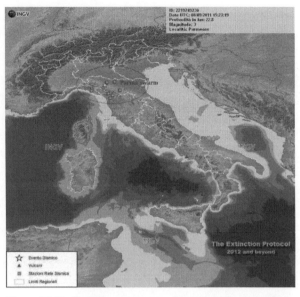

Figure 34 Earthquake storm are a feature of the Po valley

factors indicate that in the case of the Po delta, it would have extended inland beyond Monselice and that the agricultural damage caused by the exuding of deep saline water would have rendered much of the plain unusable. After a long period of drought, this was probably the final straw that broke the proverbial camel's back.

Mud volcanoes and hot springs often emit hydrogen sulphide which is extremely poisonous and has a very powerful smell of rotting eggs. The stench of mud volcanoes can cover a very large area, such as at Yellowstone Park in the USA. Marsh gas is mostly methane, which is odourless, but can contain traces of hydrogen sulphide produced from the decaying vegetation. This would be another potential source of the stench associated with the Po in ancient times. However, in terms of scale the mud volcanoes would be the most likely major source.

Earthquakes in the Po valley can also occur in a swarm, as recently as 2011 a series of at least ten small earthquakes (Richter 3) occurred over a short period of time. In a time of considerable activity, it is likely a very large number of earthquakes would occur and that some of these would be large. The effect would be to settle down the plain and to force gas and water to the surface.

The Po valley sediment sits on top of a deposit layer of salites that have hardened over geological times and date from a time when it was at sea level. These salites partly disintegrate as a result of earthquakes and enter the water table. The result of a severe earthquake would be to force salt water from the depths up to the surface rendering the land useless for agriculture.

We now need to consider other events that can occur as a result of severe earthquakes that could explain the events described in the dialogues.

Earthquakes and fault movements can cause large rivers that flow across floodplains to undergo avulsion and also cause flood plain to tilt as well as subduction where the whole or part of the plain drops a significant distance.

As we have discussed, recent studies have shown that the Po and Adige rivers have been subject to many avulsions in the past. The course of the Po river ran roughly north east during the bronze-age as is revealed by alluvial banks along the Saline-Cona route and had an avulsion in the late Bronze Age which led to a new river 20 to 30km south of the previous one. This is believed to have been an abrupt avulsion such as that of the Yellow River in 1865.

Figure 35 Avulsion in Saskatchewan River showing multiple channels that occur before the river develops a single channel

Avulsions often occur in raised rivers, that is one where alluvial banks are formed and sediment in the rivers raises them high above the surrounding floodplain, such is the case with the rivers in the Po valley. In the case of the Yellow river abnormally high rainfall led to a significant rise in river level which in turn caused breaches in the banks, within a short time the entire flow of the river had left its original course and was feeding into the surrounding floodplain. The water spouts caused by these breaches would have been horrific bearing in mind the river would be in full spate with massive flows. The surrounding plains would have been flooded to a significant depth and after this flood more would have occurred until eventually the river adopted its new course, this could have taken many years. During this time the plain would have been unusable. In addition the deposits would have made trade virtually impossible due to the damage and the changes in the water courses.

Much of the Po delta was below sea level at this time and the sea would have made an incursion inland as high tides swept into the submerged delta. This would have led to a large area becoming salt marsh. Such an avulsion of the Adige is believed to have taken place near to Monselice close to the end of the bronze-age and is given a rough date of 3000 years ago.

The Po plain is so flat that the curvature of the earth was measured by going to the top of a bell tower and observing the tops of belfries in the distance. Such flatness would make it extremely susceptible to flooding. If the surface subsided and if the top layer was washed away, it would take a considerable period of time before it returned to its former level.

It is also possible an earthquake could have caused a Tsunami, however this is less likely as there have been less instances of this in the northern Adriatic. Also, a tsunami is extremely unlikely to have permanently lowered the land level or caused the stench associated with the Eridanus (Po) or Isles of Amber referred to in later texts.

The incursion of salt water or its appearance from emission from underground water would have seriously damaged the soil productivity and would have taken a long time before it was l eached out by rainwater and floods

What we know about this time, 1200bc, is that it was a time of great upheaval. The Hittite empire collapsed as hordes of invaders swept in from the Pontic

Caspian plains probably driven by hunger. The sea peoples roamed the Mediterranean, sacking and raiding cities such as at Ugarit (where it was burnt and thus hardened and reserved some clay tablet records) and also on the Nile delta).

The Urnfield culture, which had been growing in popularity from around 1300 onwards spread rapidly with cremations replacing tumulus burials and with large number of hill forts being built and changes in weaponry with large amounts of body armour indicating a much more turbulent period in history had arrived. The collapse of the previous stable societies was probably a direct result of climate change and poor harvests which led to basic survival instinct taking over with conflicts over the limited food resources that were now available.

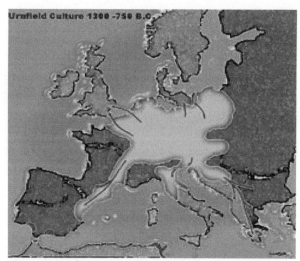

Figure 36 Urnfield culture took over from tumulus culture from 1300bc onwards and spread throughout Europe

One scenario is that a volcanic eruption which produced a huge ash cloud and ejected sulphur and carbon dioxide into the atmosphere was coupled with a sequence of earthquakes. While the ash cloud would have caused cooling for several weeks, the ash would have soon fallen to earth. However the sulphur dioxide and carbon dioxide would have had a much larger effect lasting for many years. A large amount of sulphur dioxide would have had to be sufficient to reduce the suns heating effect for long enough to produce a short term climatic cooling over several years or more. The carbon dioxide would cause the opposite effect, but reject studies by the USGS have estimated that the carbon dioxide releases would not be significant due to levels of CO2 in the atmosphere compared to the effects of the SO2 which turns to sulphuric acid. The ash cloud would have caused large amounts of rain in the short term and this rain would have been slightly acidic due to the ash. The SO2 would have caused longer term cooling. We have evidence for acidic deposits occurring in alpine lakes around this time which backs this up.

There a range of candidates for the volcano that was responsible, Hekla has often been mentioned but I believe Pinatubo is another possible candidate. Hekla produces large amounts of ash, however in the 1991 eruption of Pinatubo, the levels of sulphur dioxide were the largest ever recorded and dropped global temperatures by 1.3 degrees and lasted for around 3 years. Twenty megatons of sulphur-dioxide was emitted in this eruption.

We know that around roughly 1000bc, Pinatubo was the source of one of the largest eruptions in the last 10000 years, a colossal eruption on the same scale as Santorini and that based on the now known from data for this volcano obtained from the 1991 eruption, the amount of S02 release must have been massive and would have caused climate cooling at the time. The estimate for 18 years would be quite realistic.

The dating of the climatic event is open to some dispute. Bristlecone pine rings show a series of narrow rings dated 1021bc plus 130 minus 100bc and Irish bog oak shows an 18 year period of very reduced ring growth. Whether Hekla 3 was the cause of the climate change or not

Figure 37 Bristlecone pine tree in Yosemite. These trees are over 8000 years old and supply a history of climate throughout the ages as well as allowing radiocarbon dates to be calibrated

is actually irrelevant to the fact that during the middle of the 12th century bc a long sustained period of low growth occurred in numerous regions which is scientifically proven and must have created real problems. My view is that something must have caused this climate change and that historical records all talk of severe floods and earthquakes, darkened skies and so forth and this would fit the volcano theory.

Around 1150bc Greece saw major flooding and vast areas of land went underwater in the Hungarian plain around this time. There were several catastrophic flooding episodes at sites such as Burgaschisee, Thayngen and Federsee which led to their abandonment. This can be linked to the migration of the Bryges or Phrygians into Asia Minor. This process was probably not immediate but over a period of time. The events of around 1150bc were followed by a slightly more favourable climate which then turned much wetter and colder and by 800bc which brought an end to high level mining in the alpine regions and advancing glaciers closed off the passes such as the Brenner to trade.

Figure 38 Halley's comet as depicted been observed by Normans in the Bayeaux tapestry woven in the 11th century

The evidence for cataclysmic events appears widely in legends. The story of Ragnarok where at the end of the world the heroes ride from Valhalla in Asgard to fight the wolf in the sky and all perish is identical to a volcanic eruption or similar event, the sky darkens and there is fire and smoke everywhere but later it clears. The legend also states that at a later time items belonging to the gods could be found in the grass where they had once lived.

There is also considerable evidence for an event immediately before the floods and earthquakes that has been recorded in numerous texts at the time.

The story of Phaeton who took the reins of Helios's chariot but could not control it and crashed into the sea are identical to the description of a comet as is the story of Typhon. Again horses are pulling the Sun through the sky. In the dialog the priests refer to the story of Phaeton as a comet coming close to the earth and scorching it. If this event happened, we may assume they mentioned it in the dialogue as it was relevant to the subsequent disasters that befell Greece and Atlantis.

The most detailed description of the fall of Phaeton is given by Ovid in Metamorphoses. Phaeton begs to be allowed to drive the chariot of the Sun and Helios, his father, agrees despite grave doubts. When the horses pulling the sun feel inexperienced hands at the reins, they break out of their normal course and go out of control and plunge towards earth. Terrible fires destroy forests, cities, rivers. The Nile dries up and lands such as Libya become deserts. Earthquakes shake the earth, mountains burst into flames and ash and smoke covers the world. Zeus throws a thunderbolt and Phaeton is thrown from the chariot and lands in the Eridanus, on the banks of which the daughters of Helios mourn with tears of blood which turn into amber, the golden tears of the daughters of Helios.

Figure 39 A recent meteorite in Russia, you can see the how the ancients thought a fight was going on between two gods

Events similar to these are recorded in Egyptian inscriptions at the time of the Pharaoh Merenptah (1213 to 1203 bc) and of Ramses III (1187-1156) In the Merenptah text at Karnak dated to the 5th year of his reign it says 'Libya has become a desert...' and at Medinet Habu in texts of Ramses III 'Libya became a desert, a terrible torch hurled flame from heaven to destroy their souls and lay waste

53

their land..' and 'The Nile was dried up and the land fell victim to drought...' The comet was known as Sekhmet to the Egyptians and in the texts of Sethos II (1200-1194 bc) we read 'Sekhmnet was a circling star which spread out his fire in flames, a fire flame in his storm (Breasted)

The record in the time of Merenptah may or may not relate to these events but the later ones would definitely seem to do so. This confirms the events and gives a window for the date of the comets approach to earth. The 5th year of Merenptah's reign would be around 1208bc and in 1209bc the Hittites experienced massive food shortages, which would also place the comet at around or just before this time

Halley's Comet has been proposed as that of Phaeton. However the range of dates given for Halley's Comet passing the Earth lye in the range 1227 to 1214 bc, so unless these dates are wrong, it must be another comet or asteroid.

A huge meteorite hit Siberia in the 19th century and destroyed vast areas of woodland with trees. Diodorus Sicula recorded the myth that Phaeton had fallen to earth at the mouth of the river Po. If so that would have caused the floods and earthquakes, but this is speculation and would need further evidence to support it.

Figure 40   A huge meteorite struck the earth in Siberia in 1908 illuminated most of Russia and was seen away as far as the Caucasus. Many thought the end of the world had come

Studies of Greenland core samples from this exact time have been studied and some researchers claim that spherical particles present could only have come from an extra-terrestrial source such as a comet or asteroid. This might confirm the legend of Phaeton and similar ones from this period.

An earthquake around 1180 seems to have destroyed Troy VII and led to its abandonment. It is possible Troy VI was damaged by an earthquake but the destruction at Troy was much greater and it was burnt to the ground as with major Hittite cities nearby.

A detailed study of a number of Terramare sites just south east of Verona carried out during the 80's and 90's claimed amongst its most important discoveries that these settlements were associated with large scale hydraulic works for drainage and probably also for irrigation, much more elaborate than just ditches with systems of concentric rings and cross linked ditches. In all these excavations the subsequent phase, corresponding to the Iron-age was represented by extensive flood deposits and seems to have been a hostile environment for human settlement.   This confirms that the plain was flooded far inland after the events around 1200bc and much of it could not be reoccupied until the Etruscans moved in much later at places such as Adria.

Earthquakes in New Madrid in Missouri in 1811-12 caused large changes in ground level causing up to 12ft of subsidence. Collapsing riverbanks caused the Mississippi to change course and islands disappeared and lakes formed. The saturated bottomland soil spurted geysers of sand and black water up to 100ft into the air. The ejected water and the shaken settled sand caused severe subsidence.   The forcing out of subsurface sediment was so severe that even years later sand was covering the black soil making it useless for agricultural purposes.

In conclusion, the destruction of the city of Atlantis fits with the facts we know about major climatic events at the end of the Bronze-Age and their effect on the civilisation that inhabited the Po Venetian plain at the end of the Bronze Age. The city was covered by sea water and the area around it became salt march and centuries passed before it again became dry land. The Adige river avulsed and its delta moved north into the Venetian lagoon and the route to Europe along the passes to central Europe was cut off as the Adige and Po rivers were no longer connected close to their mouths. Cooling of the climate led to built-up of ice on the passes that rendered them unusable during the first millenium.   In the interim alternative routes to central Europe had replaced the old route and civilisation that had once occupied the Po valley disappeared from history

Chapter 3

Bronze-age Europe and Atlantis

The question now is whether in Northern Europe at this time a confederation of kingly societies existed with the degree of sophistication and scale to undertake the war that is described in the dialog.

The culture that existed during the MBA across much of Europe is called the Tumulus Culture. So called, because it buried its dead under large mounds rather than, as before, in chambered or linear tombs. This was more in line with the cult of the warrior or individual.

The Tumulus culture was itself probably a development of the Unetice culture that was spread across central Europe at the beginning of the 2nd millennium bc. The Tumulus culture thrived from roughly 1600 to 1300bc and the Urnfield culture developed from it and this continued into the Iron-age. A characteristic of the Urnfield Culture was it featured cremations rather than burials. The Terramare also cremated their dead and formed part of the Urnfield culture up to the point of their disappearance around 1100 to 1200bc.

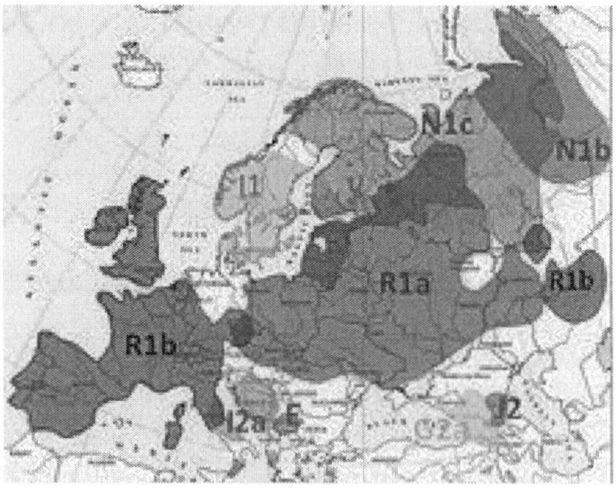

Figure 41 Map of Y-DNA chromosome haplogroups showing dominant R1b group in Europe

We know a lot more about the origin of these groups from recent DNA studies. European groups are distinguished by carrying the Y-DNA chromosome R1b haplogroup which gives the dominant paternal lineage. There are many branches or mutations of this haplogroup, but the subgroups potentially of most interest are the R1b-U152 and R-S28. These indicate the strong connections between the Urnfield areas and northern Italy which predate the Etruscans as can be seen in Fig.41.

Flat topped mounds were a feature of the Terramare culture as was building their houses on, stilts even where the ground was dry. The tumulus culture appeared across Europe from north-west Germany to the south along trade routes. Trade was established over vast areas. The Urumchi mummies in the Tarim Basin (Tibet) dated to late 2nd millennium appear to be from north European stock, with ginger or fair hair and tartan clothing.

Pins found in the Terramare culture and dated to the middle Bronze-age have an obliquely perforated globular type heads are linked to the tumulus culture and north Switzerland.

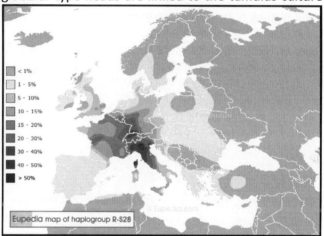

The Greeks referred to the aboriginal people in this area as the Ligurians. Aviensus in his work Ora Maritima (based on a lost work by Erastothanes) claimed the Ligurians had hegemony over the lands extending to the North Sea before they were pushed

Figure 42 The R-S28 subgroup shows how populations are linked today to common Urnfield culture ancestors

back by the Celts. Ligurian toponyms are found in Sicily. Sardinia, Corsica, along the Rhone Valley. According to Hesiod the Ligurians were one of the main barbaric peoples along with the Ethiopians and Scythians. Later on the Ligurians became associated with the Tyrrhenians then the Etruscans. Ligurians may have been a generic term for Urnfield people.

When Heracles returned from the mythical pillars he was stopped by the two sons of Poseidon, Albion and Ligures. Albion, according to myth, established himself on a remote island where he taught shipbuilding and astronomy and was made a God. He was stoned to death in a battle on the Rhine by Heracles. The pre-Roman name for Britain according to authors such as Nennius was Albion. He also noted that there had been a long line of kings in Britain before the Romans and that they had been but a footnote in the culture of this country rather than the view currently taught. This confirms co-operation between Britain and the European Urnfield people.

The Ligurians were not Celts or Iberians but probably a Dinaric race. The beaker people seem to have had their racial origins in the Alps north of the Adriatic. The beaker people settled many coastal areas of northern Europe during the late third millennium. They brought metalworking and seafaring plus a religion based on astronomy with them. They developed coastal communities and traded with the indigenous populations establishing a large scale trading network via colonies.

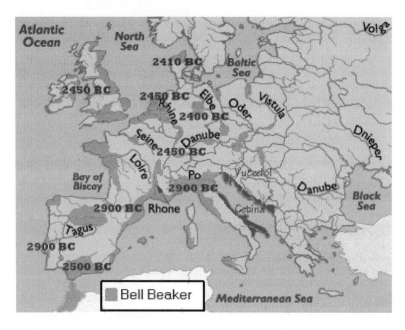

Figure 43 The beaker people were among the first sea traders. They established colonies throughout the Mediterranean and North Atlantic during the 3rd millennium and spread metallurgy throughout Europe.

Archaeology suggests that the centre of money and power in the Tumulus culture had moved more to the north-west away from its centre of gravity towards the end of the bronze-age but this does not take into account the scale of development that may have existed in the Po and Venetian lagoons.

All this suggest that as the 2nd millennium progressed, the communities throughout northern Europe became increasingly interdependent and linked together via complex trade patterns which must have required considerable interaction and we can assume that in situations in which common interests were threatened they would have joined forces to act as a confederation.

The description in the dialogues is closer to that of a state than merely a group of chiefdoms. There clearly had to be some form of central government for this whole operation to work and the regular assemblies of the kings would have provided a suitable forum for this.   However, just as in Europe today, the individual kingdoms retained independent control of local affairs.

Turning to the description of the resources of the island, we can check to see if this matches what we know would apply for the time in question.

There are references in the dialogue to elephants and to Orichalcum (mountain copper). The former could be explained by both African and Asian trade routes and the later refers to a very pure form of copper known as Chalcopyrite and even pure copper seams, which were mined in the Carpathian mountains until they ran out in around 1300bc, it was then replaced with Grey Ore which contains impurities and so later commentators such as Pausanias referred to the quality of ancient bronzes as far surpassing any of those in his time. The grey ore would have been seen as a different type of metal hence the reference to this metal no longer existing.

Figure 44 Chalcopyrite is a very good source of pure copper compared to grey ore

The other possible identity for Orichalcum could be Amber. However it seems more feasible that it was the copper from the description of its use, such as lining the floor of the temple in the acropolis in the dialog. In the Odyssey by Homer, Alcinious the King of the Phaeacians invites Odysseus to his palace which has floors covered in bronze. Clearly this was a status matter for the time period. Amber would also not be a good floor covering, copper would make sense.

We have records from 13 century Pylos of 400 artisans working in bronze with records of the operations and trade with far off lands who supplied the copper and tin. The term far off lands is used often when referring to north Europe and shows that to the Greeks it was an area which they knew little about. Herodotus confirms how sketchy their knowledge was of these areas in his History.

The dialogue refers to the island of Atlantis lying straight ahead of the pillars of Heracles but this would probably mean a ship following the coastline .

Figure 45 Phoenecian coin showing two sets of the pillars of Heracles, one has the serpent in the Ocean which refers to the Gulf Stream in the Atlantic, the other is open to debate.

The pillars of Heracles were probably trade boundary markers but the origin of a pair of pillars was much older. We know from Herodotus that a pair of pillars existed in the temple at Tyre which was dated back as far as 2800bc. Tyre has a history as old as Troy and both these places were among the first trading ports to be established. The pillars in Tyre were later copied in temples such as that of Solomon. However the pillars at Tyre were of different colours, one being gold and the other blue black stone with stars in it (possibly lapis lazuli or granite). The symbol of the Phoenicians was a pair of pillars with a snake in between. I believe the pillars represented the world pillars (ie: the two pillars on which the world was fixed one at each extreme end) and the snake was the serpent in the sea or in reality the great secret of the Phoenicians – that is the gulf-stream. The Midgard serpent is the same thing. At some stage very early on in the sea trading days of the pre-phoenicians , they must have accidently made a journey to the America's and made it back by use of the gulf stream. The gold pillar meant the Sun and the black pillar the Cosmos. Recently, cocaine was found in the nasal passage of the pharaoh Ramses II. This can only come from South America and proves the vessels were sailing to the new world and back at this time, 1250bc. The symbol of the pillars and the sea serpent simply means Trade and was also used as the symbol for the US Dollar.

Figure 46 The Nebra disk dates from this period and shows importance of astronomy in their society at this time

The serpent in the sea appears on numerous cups and artefacts in the Bronze Age cultures and they were viewed as Snake worshippers. Votive bronzes of the Villanovians as an example in the Etruscan collection in Rome show these dragons. The belief that a snake or snakes in the sea of immense size existed was clearly part of many cultures.

The dialog in Critias describes the nature of the political and legal authority in Atlantis. The island was divided into ten regions each ruled by a king with absolute authority and these kings would meet alternately every 5 or 6 years to discuss areas of mutual interest and make judgments on wrongs done by members and to make pledges. They then entered the temple of Poseidon alone where bulls roamed at large and caught one using clubs and nooses. They cut its throat over the top of the central pillar and added a clot of blood to a bowl of wine they then shared. They then swore oaths by a fire which formed part of this ceremony and after dining and carrying out business tasks donned splendid dark blue ceremonial robes and sat on the ground to perform judgments in the dark.

When the Kings of Atlantis retired to carry out judgments, they did so at night. They donned dark blue ornamental robes. Across northern Europe we have discovered numerous blue garments associated with religious events during the bronze-age and gold adornments. This includes Lunulae as well as Conus hats. These long pointed gold hats with pronounced disks were worn with the blue cloaks which would have had stars and moon symbols in gold covering them, which we now know were solar and lunar calendar charts. They were what we know as wizards, but they were real and no doubt used astronomy to convince followers that they held magical powers, such as predicting the position of the moon in the sky, eclipses and other events. If you don't do what I say I will block off the Sun, pretty effective to a less educated audience.

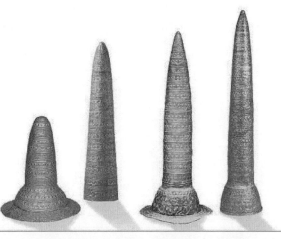

Figure 47 Gold conus hats were worn by king priests in the Urnfield culture area from around 1300bc onwards. The symbols contain all the maths required to accurately predict solar and lunar cycles over very long periods

According to historical accounts, the Areopagus assembly held in Athens was constituted along the lines of the tribunals held at this time in Egypt. Members of the assembly sat on stone benches on an open hill opposite the citadel and carried a baton as a symbol of their office. When they assembled on the hill a rope was placed in a circle around the assembly. In order that nothing should disrupt their attention they only sat in judgment at night. Demosthenes claimed that no one ever complained of injustice in the acts of the assembly.

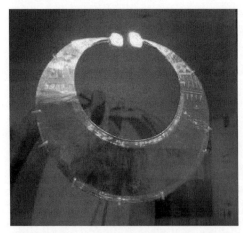

Figure 48 Many Lunulae have been found in the uk and Northern Europe and are obviously ceremonial and linked to the moon

The description of the temple in the acropolis says it contained a statue of the god standing on a chariot drawn by six horses with a hundred Nereids around it. In fact there have been many similar votive works recovered from graves in Europe dated to the Bronze-age. The chariot often appears more like a cart and sometimes is drawn by geese or ducks and features many animals or people on the chariot. However the description fits very well with items that have been archaeologically recovered and can be seen by anyone. The Trondheim sun disk is another connected example from Denmark, the idea is much the same. Whether the God depicted was Poseidon or Apollo is open to debate. Apollo, the Sun god is pulled by horses through the sky as the Sun undertakes it daily journey from East to West. This myth is a very ancient one in north European culture.

Figure 49   The Trondheim sun disk. This religious artefact from Denmark dates from the bronze-age and shows the solar disk being pulled by horse(s) across the sky. One form of Poseidon was the horse.

It is true that horses were associated with Poseidon, who brought them over the sea, but he was also more associated with the bull and later with the sea. Later statues of Poseidon show him riding a bull. Gods were normally depicted astride their previous animal form in antiquity. The bulls in the temple and the bull sacrifice would fit with the cult of Poseidon.

The mixing of Bull's blood with wine in a cauldron from which drinking cups are filled is attested as a ritual carried out in antiquity in northern Europe and is a form of blood oath, which is very ancient.

Cauldrons from the Villanova culture show dragons or serpents leaping up around the bowl to its rim.

They have their mouths open and if we looked at them from a purely observatory point of view we would associate them with crocodiles when they are hunting in the water. Interestingly, the Egyptians considered a crocodile a serpent. They considered serpents had many forms and this was one of them and a crocodile was absolutely a serpent in one form. This again shows that a dragon can have aspects of a crocodile built into to it as this was also a snake in the minds of the ancients.

Figure 50 A Villanovian culture cauldron from early iron age showing serpents around the bowl

The capitol of the island is described as being constructed as a sequence of alternating rings of water and land with the acropolis in the centre, we know the Terramare built large canals which were fed from river in the Po plain and we also know that along the coast of Northern Europe cities such as Amsterdam and Bruges feature similar designs although these were constructed relatively recently. However, canals were widely in use in antiquity. One of the oldest referred to is in Herodotus' description of the building of the pyramids. He records that when they were finished they were clad in white marble (which we know is true) and that a canal of huge size stretched from the Nile to the site at Giza and that artificial lakes fed by this canal with gardens surrounded the pyramids. The pyramids were constructed around 2300bc. In fact the oldest major irrigation systems are recorded in Mesopotamia where by 2500bc canals connected the major cities and acted to irrigate the land. A tablet uncovered at Nippur dated to 1550bc shows a complex canal network in regular use.

We only have to look at Venice, Amsterdam, Bruges and other cities to see that even today cities based on canals and a circular pattern are a feature of coastal European towns.

Figure 51 Amsterdam, like Bruges, Venice and other cities around Europe is constructed about canals on a roughly circular pattern.

The hill he fortified in the central island was near the sea, it is one part of the island of Atlantis from this text and also it does not say Ocean. If we assume the first island was the Po valley and the hill somewhere near the delta then the other islands were populated later by his children. Again this myth refers to colonies that were set up by the original kingdom. These events would have been a far distant recollection of colonisations far in the past. So we should look for colonies that could have been founded from this region is other parts of Europe. We do not need to look far to find the answer. As trade by sea and copper working took hold in the latter part of the 3rd millennium, a new group of colonists appears on the scene on Northern Europe which can be distinguished by the nature of their burials and by the structures they built. We call them the beaker people because they buried their dead with a special type of beaker. However, more importantly, they appear to have brought metalworking and long distance sea trade to the shores of northern Europe. They are distinguished by the skull type. Unlike the indigenous population they had Brachocephalic skulls (round skulls) rather than Dolichocephalic (long skulls). Ai more detailed study assessed these as Dinaric type skulls from southern alpine regions. The beakers could have been drinking vessels but were used to smelt copper ores and maybe this was why they were included in the burials.

The various elements of the bell beaker culture seem to have fused first in the lower Rhine region according to recent research. The change for the previous culture was a shift to the cult of the individual with warrior burials under tumuli associated with weapons such as daggers. Formerly you had linear and chambered tombs more associated with farming communities with the absence of weapons.

Figure 52 bell shaped beaker to which the people buried with them were given the name Beaker People the beaker was used in life for wine and maybe also in metal smelting

This would not be surprising, as the Balkans had been the centre of metalworking for a considerable time and bronze working seems to have spread out from the Carpathian area in antiquity. We know from the ice man that contrary to previous thinking, bronze axes were in use back around 3000bc in the Alps as he was carrying a bronze axe in his bag when he was found 5000 years later.

We know quite a lot about the Beaker people, they starting to spread throughout the north European region late in the 3rd millennium as shown in Fig 43, establishing coastal colonies for trade, metal working and building megalithic structures such as stone henges.

The Beaker people were sun worshippers from examples including the moving of stones at Stonehenge to realign with the sun as opposed to the moon which had formerly been worshipped by the Neolithic indigenous population. The Athenians worshipped the Moon, their protagonists worshipped the Sun. From early times (Burl) they buried with the skulls facing north in a highly ritualistic fashion.

We are told the Atlanteans were worshippers of Poseidon. Poseidon was a god in various guises, a sea god, a horse god and a bull god. He was the giver of horses and ships with sails, the sea bull and was depicted as a god holding a trident sitting on a bull. It seems his oldest form was a bull god as generally an

Figure 53 Bronze-age bull god from Ugarit possibly Baal

animal on which a god stands represents his primitive form. The worship of bulls is one of the oldest forms and stretches back as far as Catal Huyuk around 8000 years ago. It was prevalent throughout Northern Europe and the Mediterranean. It was linked to simple farming communities and bulls skulls appear on numerous ancient sites. Stonehenge contains evidence of bull cults. Aubrey holes lie within a high bank with a ditch marked by four ox skulls. A long barrow at Beckhampton row in Wiltshire (before 2000bc) has three ox skulls buried in a line along the ridge. They had probably originally been placed on poles. Morris dancers still carry a bulls head on a pole. At Irthlingborough in Northamptonshire, at least 185 ox skulls were found overlaying a beaker period burial site. The Minotaur in Crete is a later example and it is likely (as in the UK) that the bull skull was worn during religious ceremonies. There was also a clear link between the all-powerful mother goddess and the bull and also between the bull cult and kingship. The bull cult may have been associated with fertility and strength and clearly a male god. The horse cult probably followed that of the bull as the horse became increasing more important. Finally, the sea- god evolves as trade takes over as the dominant occupation. We know that Poseidon was linked to Europe. In the Odyssey the children of Poseidon were Giants and Cyclopes. The Cyclopes were smiths who covered one eye as a safety measure when working). The Giants were

Figure 54 Sacred bull effigy from Knossos in Crete

north Europeans, even today very large people inhabit some parts of Europe and to the small Greeks who averaged barely over five foot they would have been giants. In another section the Cyclopes tell Odysseus 'the Cyclopes have no fear of Zeus'. In most of the Greek mythology Zeus and Poseidon are in conflict and each considers himself superior.

The Athenian's had to choose between Poseidon and Athena, according to their legends and this took place around the time of Erectheus, which is the

same time as the war with Atlantis. They chose Athena (the mother goddess) and rejected Poseidon. Athena was probably depicted as an owl in pre Hellenistic times and was like Sophia linked to wisdom (the ancient sign for wisdom and knowledge). Sophia is of course Isis by another name and Isis the sister of

Figure 55 Horns of consecration from Knossos in Crete where bull worship was practised

Osiris is a version of the mother goddess. The black Artemis is another old fertility goddess who like Osiris is linked to the cycle of the seasons. The important point is that the roles of the gods often changes and the importance of the roles likewise rises and falls with the passage of time. The ceremony undertaken by the kings of Atlantis as described in the dialog fits with what one would expect in the European culture of the time, the sacrifice of the bull over the pillar being a very old tradition that had not changed for a very long time. The mixing of the blood in a bowl of wine is another ritual that was undertaken in northern Europe. Cauldrons such as the Guldstrop cauldron were probably used in such ceremonies, Herodotus refers to the blood oaths of the Scythians where unlike the Greeks, he says, they mixed their own blood in a cup before undertaking an oath. This practice was common in the Mediterranean and Europe at this time and we still talk of blood oaths today.

The dialog tells that the laws were written onto gold plates which were dedicated along with their robes as a record. The presence of writing in bronze-age Europe is a hotly debated subject. If they had writing it was not the type of writing we would recognise. If anything it would have been a cryptic form. It seems that to maintain a high level of trade at large distances they could not have solely relied on memory of

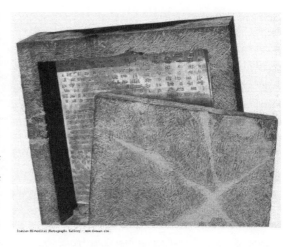

Figure 56 Gold plates from Persepolis at time of Darius with records inscribed onto them

passing of information down the line. It would have been a cryptic form where symbols placed in particular positions represented concepts. It would have

Figure 57 Linear A plate from Crete dated before 1450bc

been more like secret codes not readily understood by the uninitiated. We know writing was placed on copper and gold plates in the middle-east long before this time but that of course is not proof it happened here but does show it is possible and that they were probably aware of this process through trade. The Mohenjo Daro wrote extensively on copper plates in the early 2nd millennium.

Their symbols which also appear on seals have been decoded. Some display a divinity with three faces, horns on his head, wearing elaborate torques and a belt. The same figure appears as Cernunnos in Gaul. The ancient Britons and Europeans (such as Danes and Sardinians) wore helmets with bull's horns on them. These were not a weapon but more likely a sign of belonging to the cult of the bull god, the wearing of the horns would have

69

Figure 58 Linear B text sometimes called cattle track appeared from 1450bc onwards and similar to Linear A but identified by Michael Ventris as an early form of Greek

given them strength from wearing the symbol of the all-powerful god just as the Crusaders wore the cross and so on. Carvings on megalithic monuments contain a number of chief elements which appear throughout Europe wherever megalithic monuments appear.

Rebus symbols are the stage between proto writing and full writing which leads to syllabic systems followed by consonantal (Egyptian) and finally alphabetic writing. Syllabic systems would include Linear B. In Crete, Linear a writing was used up until around the time of the Mycenaen period when it was replaced by Linear B which is a form of Greek. Linear A has not been deciphered.

There were also many other ways of passing information. According to Herodotus, Darius gave the Greeks a thong with sixty knots in it. He told them to undo one every day and if he was not back before they were all undone to return home. Such systems where common but obviously leave no physical record. Tallies are another example, in trade in the Mediterranean a pot would be made containing a number of beads, it would be sent with the consignment. On arrival the pot would be broken and the beads counted to tally

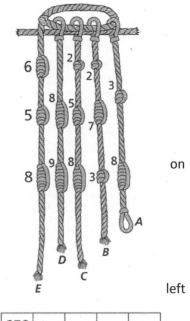

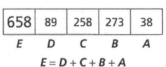

658	89	258	273	38
E	D	C	B	A

$$E = D + C + B + A$$

Figure 59 Inca system of knots used to keep records showing example of simple summation of numbers

with the quantity of goods. It could also identify the nature of the goods as well if required. This was a very effective method to keep track of goods being traded over long distances. The British Treasury used tally sticks to record receipts from 1100 to 1834. In fact the Inca civilisation is a good example of an empire being run without writing (they used knotted arrangements of rope and cords to keep track). In conclusion, it does not require writing to run an empire and it would have been perfectly possible to operate with alternative

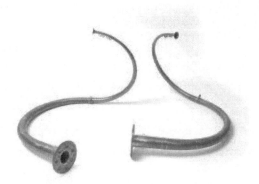

systems. The writing described could have been cryptic and restricted to a very small group and so there are no probably records of it. The symbols used on the complex gold object uncovered would have been significant but cannot be deciphered as they probably relate to concepts which are lost to history.

Figure 60 A pair of Lurs from Denmark, These horns were used at ceremonies and possibly in war and produce a loud sound which can be heard over distance

In the dialog an allotment had to provide a sixth part of the equipment used for war which included a sixth part of equipment for a war chariot with horses and riders, a combatant with light shield, two hoplites, two archers, two slingers, three stone throwers and three javelin men and four sailors. Large number of swords, shields, javelin heads have been found over the years as well as some examples of longbows, which had been in use before 3000bc, as shown by examples discovered.

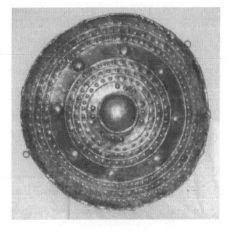

Figure 61 Round shield of middle late bronze age from Scotland. This type of shield was typical throughout europe and

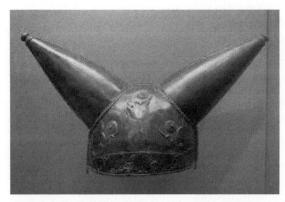

Figure 62 The Waterloo helmet, called after where it was discovered is an example of a late bronze age helmet

Instruments of the time used in battle and at religious ceremonies would have included bull roarers and lurs. The Sardinians shown among the Sea Peoples at Medinet Habu have round shields and helmets with horns. Sword styles developed from thrusting types into longer slashing type swords in the latter part of the Bronze Age and chariots appeared, it seems the Egyptians copied their chariots from those found in Europe. Across much of Europe the weapons bear remarkable similarities indicating strong connections with the flow of ideas and practices.

Southern expansion (some argue from the Tagus Valley in Portugal) led to enclaves in the middle of the third millennium at Cadiz, in the Golfe de Lion and in the Po valley. Northern expansion covered Armorica, Ireland, Britain and Jutland. Sardinia, Sicily and Corsica plus the Balearic islands were also colonised. In almost all cases the colonies were on the sea coast and when inland were close to large rivers. The colonies in central Europe would have followed the major river trade routes linking regions together. The map of the beaker culture areas shows a connected group of enclaves close to the sea or rivers and in essence looks just like a group of islands connected with trade. In fact it is a good way to describe the Atlantis confederation.

Figure 63 Bronze age weapons from Romania of styles common across Europe during bronze age

The dialog describes the political and legal authority that operated in the state of Atlantis as follows 'Their arrangement for the distribution of authority and office were the following. Each of the ten kings had absolute power and authority in his own region and city, over persons and in general laws and could punish and execute at will. But their distribution of power between them and their mutual relations were governed by Poseidon, enshrined in laws on an orichalcum pillar in the temple of Poseidon in the middle of the island'

We can sense from this that these kingdoms shared a number of things including a common religious heritage based on Poseidon. The rise of megalithic monuments coincides with the arrival of beaker peoples in many places. It is fairly certain that the Sun was the main focus of religion up until their arrival as evidence from barrows and sites such as Stonehenge suggest. However you get a sense, which I have experienced in places such as Avebury, that stone circles took over the old sites, possibly forcefully and replaced them, in the same way Christianity did with the old religious sites here.   While there is no complete consensus as to the function of monuments such as stone circles there is general agreement that they concern the stars, moon and sun and concern matters such as the cycle of life and death and fertility which govern our lives. If there is an alignment of the circles it seems generally to be towards the west where the Sun sets, but beyond this a section of the sky containing combinations of solar, lunar and star movements may have been sacred.

The Nebra disk confirms that star positions were of significance to cultures in north Europe during the Bronze Age. Fibonacci numbers may suggest the universe does not work off a denary system, we use it because of our fingers but it is not absolute.

The temple referred to in the dialogue was one stadia in length (600ft) and a half in width. It was barbaric in appearance and had pinnacles and pillars. It had an inner enclosed sanctum with a pillar in the middle. Stonehenge consists of several circles of stones and henges. The innermost bluestone circle is around 100ft with another circle 300ft and a henge of outer diameter 600ft. A covered area probably existed in the centre. This shows that a temple of the dimensions and style given in the dialogue is consistent with buildings that existed in North Europe in the Bronze Age. It certainly could fit a megalithic structure similar to a Stone Circle although this culture did not seem reach Italy.

Figure 64 Stonehenge aerial view clearly shows the five trilithons in the centre surrounded by the bluestones

Beyond astronomical uses, there is evidence of a bull cult at Stonehenge. A ring of posts in the Aubrey stones lie within a high bank the limits of which are marked by Ox skulls. Cup marks also appear on the stones which clearly had some religious significance. It is quite likely that writing was restricted to the use of symbols in a religious context that was extremely ancient and so the archaic nature of these symbols does not necessarily reflect the sophistication of the society. One only has to observe our world today to see this is so.

We now know that the Aubrey stones at Stonehenge were used as calendars to predict events such as eclipses but also to fix other important dates during the year such as the winter and summer solstices and other longer term events. At Stonehenge in Wiltshire it has been shown how complex the calculations were when the Aubrey stones were used in conjunction with the rest of this predictive instrument. Its use was no doubt both practical and religious. However, by the time of Atlantis most of these structures had fallen into disuse. One reason may have been that they lost their accuracy due to the earth's precession as the centuries rolled by and it was not easy to keep on recalibrating when stones weighing tons needed to be moved around. Another reason would be the rise of cult of the individual and the replacement of old gods by ones resembling man allowing the king or ruler who prevailed to be associated with divinity. In order to maintain hierarchies in these larger societies it must have been important for the ruler to present himself as superior and elevated from his subjects, with the risk of familiarity breeding contempt, showing off power in displays of pomp and wealth would have been required to keep the social order in place.

So if the Atlantis dialogues are based essentially on fact, the consequences are considerable as they are virtually the only written record of European society in the Bronze Age and reshape our views on the type of society that existed at that time.

Figure 65 The Phaestos disk from Crete dates to the bronze-age and is the first example of signs being stamped onto clay in a manner similar to printing. The signs have not been deciphered and its origin is unknown, Dorians have been proposed and many signs are similar to objects relating to northern Italy which had an almost identical culture

Returning to the theme of the absence of written records and the level of sophistication of a society. Even into Roman times the Druids chose to commit almost all their knowledge to memory rather than write it down, even though they could have. In the middle Bronze-age written records were relatively rare and restricted to a very few elite members of society. Even into relatively modern times illiteracy rates in Europe were very high, but this did not prevent large scale operations from being undertaken. It is also apparent that symbols or logo graphics were used instead of alphabetic or phonetic writing for communication at this time (Linear A was in use in Crete at this time) Linear B came into use around 1400bc and Cuneiform was in use aiming the Hittites and Egypt used hieroglyphs. Writing was certainly more prevalent in the middle-east, but examples such as the Phaestos disk, where characters were stamped show that other systems we know little about also were in use. The important point about the dialog is it tells us that the societies in Europe at this time were well structured and organised at a higher level than previously accepted.

The middle Bronze Age was characterised by a change from simple agrarian societies to much more complex societies with defined levels of social distinction which arose as trade and manufacturing took became the major sources of individual wealth. In the Ore Mountains smelting began early in the 2nd millennium and bronze manufacture was established. The large markets

included Egypt, Assyria and the Hittite Empire. Transport by land was slow compared to transport by sea. Even in the UK until the 19th century, it was much quicker to take a packet boat from London to Edinburgh than to take a stagecoach. The closest port linking the European centres of metallurgy to the major markets in the Mediterranean would have been those in the north Adriatic.

Figure 66 Open cast mining in the Ore mountains in South Germany where much of the copper in the MBA was mined

The problem once the goods were loaded onto boats was to get them safely to the end customer. The Mediterranean was littered with pirates. The Tyrrhenians were well known pirates into antiquity and made travel down the east coast of Italy a risky process. However, the Minoans had cleared much of the Eastern Mediterranean of pirates and the Phoenicians (or more correctly at this time Tyrrhenians) also kept control of trade along the Levant and Turkish coastline probably as far as Troy and the Hellespont.

The societies in South Eastern Europe in modern day Romania and Bulgaria were mostly chiefdoms with small rural settlements of 10 to 50 people who led a sedentary existence. These small villages were widely dispersed and there appears to be little evidence of large scale communities. In fact in the Voyage of the Argo, Apollonius comments on the backward nature of these areas at this time.

Centres of metal production also existed in the Caucasian mountain region at the far Eastern end of the Black Sea. The voyage of the Argo was partly undertaken to visit Colchis was allegedly based here and the legend of the golden fleece records the discovery of how gold was extracted by these people from rivers using a fleece as is still done until recent times.

Figure 67 Replica of the Argo in which Jason and the Argonauts are said to have travelled the Black Sea, and far up the Danube returning to the Mediterranean. Boats up to 20m long have been found across Europe

At the end of the 2nd millennium, metals were arriving from this region into the Mediterranean from the Black Sea via the Hellespont. It was the threat to Mycenaean business by the Trojans that led to the Trojan War. As Herodotus says 'no one went to war over the abduction of a woman' and continues to say that it was nevertheless 'the Phoenicians who were to blame'

I believe that the Phoenicians working with the Trojans had opened up a supply line to Egypt which cut out the Mycenaeans and so led to the war. The Mycenaeans had gained control of trade over most of the Eastern Mediterranean by this time and needed to protect their interests. The journey of the Argo would have taken place after the Trojan War and the disasters that followed it. This was the first time the Greeks had ventured into the Black Sea, which was why it was so well remembered. They also explored the old trade routes in the now sparsely inhabited regions after the collapse of the Hittite empire and also that of the Atlanteans.

Herodotus in his Histories says that Colchis had been colonised by troops left behind from the Egyptian pharaoh Sesostris campaigns and Apollodorus state that the Colchians gave Jason stone tablets made before the flood of Deucalion, showing ancient trade routes throughout Europe and the Black Sea, which had been produced by the Egyptians. The known list of Pharaohs does not contain a Sesostris. However we know the Hyksos occupied the delta from roughly 1800bc to 1550bc and that they were expelled by Ahmose I in around 1550bc. The pharaoh Thutmose III (1479 to 1425) was the pharaoh responsible for building the giant Egyptian Empire. He won victories throughout the middle-east and into Africa as far as Nubia. He crossed the Euphrates and defeated the Mitanni, whose empire stretched north as far as Colchis.

We can assume that during the Hyksos occupation, the Egyptians did not venture out of Egypt into Europe of Asia and that unless the Egyptians referred to by Herodotus were actually the Hyksos, then it is likely that it would have been after 1550 and before 1400bc (as Akenhaten and his father definitely did not venture deep into Asia). The most likely candidate would be Thutmose III, who undoubtable sent expeditions far and wide ahead of his military campaigns.

Figure 68 Cecrops receives Ericthonious from Athena passed to her by Gaia. Note the serpent tail on Cecrops

It is also interesting that Cecrops and Pelops among other travelled from Egypt around 1550bc after the defeat of the Hyksos. Again, writers could have referred to the Hyksos as Egyptians or otherwise the freeing of the delta could have meant that the Egyptians would have moved out take over the trade routes the Hyksos had operated and so sent expeditions out to build links with the new trading partners they had inherited.

The Hyksos were an Asiatic people who settled in the delta around 1800bc and built a capital city, Avaris, in the Sais nome (nome was a division of Egypt similar to a county). They brought bronze weapons and better chariots (or at least better versions) to the Egyptians. They also introduced new gods such as Astarte and Rhephos and adopted Seth as their main god. They practised horse burials, introduced Zebu cattle.

The harbour at Avaris could hold at least 300 ships and buildings excavated show similarities with Minoan ones, with wall paintings similar to those at Knossos in Crete. Various origins have been speculated, but the most likely appears to around Palestine, Syria, Lebanon coasts and Cyprus. We can assume they traded by sea extensively, as trade from the delta to places such as Byblos had been undertaken from far back into the 3rd millennium.

One interesting fact about Sais, is that it held the yearly festival of Neith and that this was mostly an Osirian type ceremony (death and rebirth), but that a cow sacred to Hathor which was said to contain the soul of Neith was paraded through the streets during this festival. The link between bull worship and Neith being clear with Neith being the dominant god as in the case of Athena and Poseidon.

The Atlanteans had decided to seize the moment after the eruption at Santorini had damaged the ability of the Minoans to regulate the seas and had extended their direct influence as far as the Eastern and Southern Mediterranean. However, the Athenians challenged them and the

Figure 69 Nuraghe fortresses in Sardinia date from middle bronze-age and there are hundreds of ruined examples. With walls up to 10m high they were impregnable

confederation we refer to as the Mycenaean Empire took over from the Minoans. They then faced new challenges from the Trojans. The fortifications at the Greek Cities such as Mycenae, in Sardinia and in Istria and elsewhere, testify to the dangers involved in this process of trade, the accumulation of wealth had led to the rise of robbery and piracy throughout the region.

The presence of large forts on hilltops in Sardinia occurs around 1500bc along

with the building of numerous furnaces to process the copper and lead resources in the island. This culture just as those along the Atlantic seaboard and in the Po and Veneto valleys, were developments from the earlier Beaker culture. The Nugaric forts are some of the few large stone structures that remain and their size and scale matches

Figure 70 An accurate reconstruction of a Nuraghe fortress. The Sharda among the sea peoples shown in carvings on the walls at Medinet Habu belonged to these fortresses

that at Mycenae and Troy this time.

In conclusion it seems a group of interdependent and socially connected states existed at the end of the Bronze Age throughout much of Europe. They shared a common cultural ancestry and traded extensively with the Mediterranean. The largest centre of trade naturally lay at the mouth of the Adige River where it entered the Adriatic. These societies left virtually no written records and few buildings as the materials they used were not lasting.

In future I will use MBA for Middle Bronze Age and RBA for Late Bronze Age in the text.

Chapter 4

The location of the acropolis and city

We have been told a number of things in the dialogues about the location of the acropolis and city. That they lie close to each other connected by a road and bridge, that they lie close to the sea at around 50 stadia and midway along the length of the plain. We also know that there are hot and cold springs nearby. We are told the city was connected to the sea by a canal 300ft width length 50 stadia (9km) in length from the sea and 100ft deep.

The mid-point of the coastline of the Po valley and Venetian plain is roughly east of the southern tip of the Eugenai hills. We know from extensive recent studies of the alluvial plain in the delta that in the MBA the Adige river ran in an line from the town of Este marked by the Montagnana-Este alluvial ridge just south of the Rock of Monselice when it turned south east along a path marked by the Bagnoli ridge to join the Po river close to the town of Agna. The two rivers then shared the same outflow into the Adriatic. The distance from the Rock of Monselice along the Adige to the point where it joined the Po was around 16km (80 stadia).

Figure 71 The Adriatic at Torcello Laguna shows the shoal mud in the lagoons that has always been a feature of this region

Figure 72 Adige River at Verona is over 200ft wide at this point and has been altered by embankments to make it more usable

The Adige is the longest river in Italy and so it would seem safe to assume that the point at which it joined the Po close to the Adriatic would be considered as the coast. The journey from this point would have been up the Adige which would be defined as the river on which both the city and acropolis stood. So the city would have been 50 stadia from this junction. This is an approximate distance so anything up to 10km would be reasonable. This would place the city which had a diameter of roughly a distance of 2km or more from the acropolis, which is believable.

The Adige at Verona is around 200ft wide with stone walling on each bank to protect against surges in the river. The alluvial ridges along the Adige could have been modified to turn it into a canal and so its width would be around the figure given in the dialog for access to the city. It currently widens to around 300ft just south of Monselice on its present course. The description of the canal to the sea at 300ft would make sense if the river was modified by embankments. The depth at 100ft would seem to be an error as often happened in classical times as depth measurements were highly inaccurate.

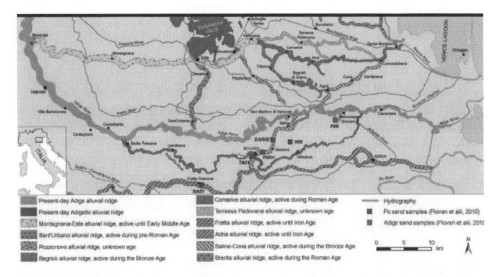

Figure 73 Extensive recent studies of the north eastern Po valley have detailed the presence of ancient alluvial ridges which plot the history of the course of the Adige over time and indicate dates at which major avulsions occurred.

After the avulsion of the Adige shortly after 1200bc, the new river followed a course further north into the marsh area of the delta marked by the Conselve alluvial ridge. The deactivation of the Saline-Cona Po branch around 1000bc through the avulsion at Rovigo led to the southward shift of the Po delta and the Adige built its own delta from 1000bc up until Roman times in the southern Venice lagoon prograding onto the previous northern Po delta lobe.

The Po changed course and moved from a path marked by the Saline-Cona ridge to the Adria alluvial ridge, Where the Etruscans built a town in the Iron age. The present course of the Adige emerges further south as shown in the figure above.

It is worth noting that the avulsion meant that the former route up the Adige off the Po had been effectively closed and that journeying up the Po would take you along the Po valley towards the south and away from the Adige. The new inlet for the Adige was much further north and among marshes and mudflats. The effects of the Avulsion of these rivers and the flooding of the plain would have created significant problems in navigating the Adige. The voyage of the Argo probably followed the Po and not the Adige.

The Venetian lagoon is the only survivor of a system of estuarine lagoons that extended from Trieste to Ravenna in Roman times. It is still the largest wetland area in the Mediterranean. The lagoon comprises 8 percent dry land, 11 percent water and 80 percent mudflats, shallows and salt marshes. The tide in the north Adriatic is also among the highest in the Mediterranean at around 1m. There are still remnants of the other lagoons at Ravenna and Comacchio. During the iron-age these lagoons would have made travel extremely difficult, especially if they were in a quasi-stable state and we know that there were other evulsions during the iron-age.

Figure 74 Nasa photograph of the Venetian lagoon shows clearly the mud flats and complex arrangement of channels within the lagoon

The area around Ferrara is also known for springs and the Po valley has both cold and hot springs at numerous locations, as mentioned in the dialogue. There are very famous springs at Abano Terme and Battaglia near Padua which are close to a small hill in the Po valley. The hot springs were famous in Roman times and water was conveyed over significant distances. The Battaglia springs are only around 2km or just over a mile from the Rocca Monselice. The old Etruscan towns of Este and Adria (from which the Adriatic gets its name) are just south of Padua and on the main outflows of the Po river. Battaglia Terme is the more southerly spring town in this area today and in ancient times a spring could have been located at the acropolis as described in the dialog.

The Etruscans built Adria after the river there had ceased to be the main outflow of the Po, when they built Adria it was a harbour on the coast of the Adriatic. It now lies 22km inland from the sea. We could speculate that the sea was another 5km west at around 1300bc which would have meant that Monselice was only a few miles from the coast – a distance of 8km or 5miles would be quite realistic. This confirms the description given in Critias.

The Montagna Este alluvial ridge shows the course of the Po during the bronze-age and into roman times. During the early part of the 1st millennium bc a town was built at Montagna far up the Adige and over a hundred years later another town was built at Este, before the Etruscans arrived and built the major town of Adria on the Po river. This became the largest port in the north Adriatic and handled most of the Amber and other goods arriving from northern Europe. It is interesting that trade along the Udine did not develop and this may be accounted for lack of access. Adria also lay on the Po River and not on the Adige which now flowed into the Venetian lagoon. The Adige and Po Rivers ran on separate courses after an avulsion at Rovigo.

The Etruscan Adria is buried at least 2 to 3metres into the mud below the present city. So any buildings from the Bronze Age would probably lie at least 4m deep as we know that they lay under the water just after their destruction around 1200bc so they would be another 2m below the Etruscan remains.

The fact that a town was built at Montagna and then moved to Este might indicate that the region around Este was unsuitable for a town around 1000bc and that the new town had to be built as far up the Adige as Montagna.

The Venetian lagoon is very shallow and less than waist deep in large areas. It makes no difference whether it is 3 or 50 ft deep as to reducing its population carrying capacity. So one can see how the flooding of the Po plain even if to a very low depth would prevent agricultural use and cause abandonment of the area.

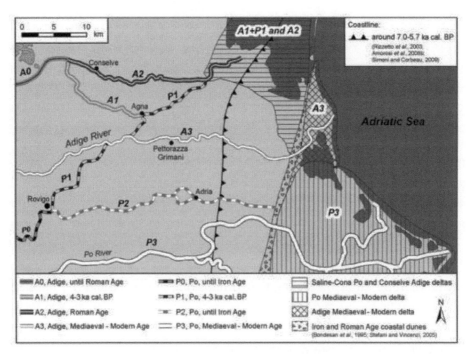

Figure 75 This diagram shows the course of the river Adige at various times in history with A1 its route until the avulsion changed it to A2 in the late bronze age The distance of the Adige from the rock of Monselice to where it joins the Po is around 16km. (Ruth Whitehouse)

Further to this, recent paleogeographical studies of the Po delta and southern Venetian lagoon area confirm that during the bronze-age the shoreline was further inland than today and that paleochannels show that the river Adige ran close to the Eugenei hills to the north of the Po valley and formed a semicircle towards the north touching Monselice at its top.

The description of the city is that a central area was 5 stadia in diameter surrounded by a canal 1 stadium in width, this was followed by a ring of land 2 stadia wide itself enclosed in a canal 2 stadia wide. This in turn was surrounded by a ring of land 3 stadia wide enclosed by a ring of water 3 stadia wide from which it was possible to go to the sea. The total diameter is 27 stadia or around 5km or 3miles in diameter.

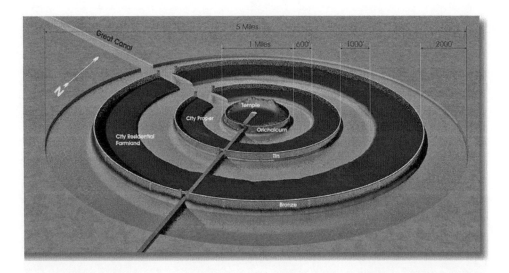

Figure 76 The simplified plan of the central city as given in Plato's account. There are three areas of land surrounded by three rings of water connected to the sea by a cana.l Dimensions shown are overestimates

The last canal would be 1800 feet wide according to this account. The overall size of the city seems reasonable but the widths of the canals would seem to be overestimates. If we look at similar cities such as Amsterdam we would expect the width of the canals to be smaller. It may be that the writers wrote down these dimensions without distinguishing them or that the widths of the canals given referred to only certain points on their circumference.

However, as this city was on a major trade route and a port connected to the sea it would have been built by a river close to the sea. So the outer ring is more likely mostly a river and a canal dug part around to finish the encirclement the town to complete. The width of the ring does not have to be 3 stadia all way round so this would fit the description. It states the canal to the sea was constructed on huge dimensions – but this could easily refer to the manmade alteration of the existing river in places to suit its purpose as a port. The inner rings being much smaller and not connected with the sea could well have been dug out. The dimensions are again approximate – so the widths can be maxima and it is doubtful if the structure was a precise circle, the dialog is aimed at giving an idea so the tolerances can be quite large without affecting the essence of what is being conveyed.

In the text it states that the first thing they did was to build a bridge over the rings around the original hill where Poseidon had lived and connect it to the palace that was in the main town. The palace and town were presumably in close proximity so we are looking for a small hill maybe 5 stadia in size (half a mile diameter) in this area of the Po valley.

Figure 77 The Rock of Monselice as it is today, once the ancient acropolis of the kingdom of Atlantis with commanding views over access to the Adige and so to mainland Europe

There is one such hill, that fits this description and that is Monselice la Rocca. Today it has a castle built on its top as it is an excellent location from which to view the surrounding Po valley as it must have been in antiquity. We know the city of Atlantis was destroyed by earthquakes and floods, but the original hill must still remain as this would not have disappeared. This appears to be the sole candidate that fits the description and also looks as you would expect. In Critias the narrative we hear '....to make the hill whereon she dwelt impregnable he (Poseidon) broke it off all round' (Loeb pp231). He then encircled the original acropolis with rings of water and land of equal width. We are therefore certainly looking for a small rocky hill with steep sides which fits the rock of Monselice perfectly.

During the bronze-age the Adige ran a course just below the rock of Monselice and it would have provided an excellent control point for the river close to its outlet into the sea. The view from the top would have given a clear view over the town and river far into the distance and also provided a natural defensive position. The town would have most likely been located on the inland side of the Adige for defensive reasons and would have been overlooked the Rock.

At a distance of 2 miles south slightly east we have the visible signs of a rectangular structure and also around it numerous lines and parts of rings consistent with the traces of former canals and structures between the communities of Rovigana II and Stortola.

These would have been about 5 miles inland at the time of the war referred to. The dialog gives the dimensions of the central island as 5 stades (about 3000ft) surrounded by a ring of water one stadium in width (600ft) this in

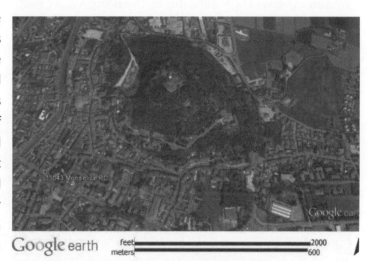

Figure 78 An aerial view of the rock clearly shows why it was chosen as a fortress in ancient time, but too small

turn was encircled by a ring of land 2 stadia wide itself encircled by another ring of water 2 stadia wide followed by a ring of land 3 stadia and water 3 stadia, Into total the width would have been 27 stadia or between 2 and 3 miles in diameter. So the distance to Monselice Rock would have been around 2 miles and from the outer ring less than a mile, possibly half a mile.

This is quite a large town for the times. A small town 2 or 3 miles in diameter would certainly have a population of 10 to 20,000 people. It is not particularly large as city for its time but not insignificant.

From all the evidence and the dialog we can place the location of the city south east of Monselice Rock close to the original course of the river in the area around the small village of Pozzonova. An initial inspection of the area from satellite images shows clear evidence of works in this area that could be relevant. However, as it is clear that the majority of the buildings were made of wood it is unlikely anything remains of these. As the city was destroyed by earthquakes and floods it is clear very little if any physical evidence could remain and if anything is there to be found it will be buried very deep.

There is an undated alluvial ridge called the Pozzonovo ridge which runs directly from Monselice though the middle of Pozzonovo and on to the Adige. Whether this was operating during the Bronze Age awaits further investigation. However the Bagnoli ridge would have touches on a circle the diameter of the city centred at Pozzonovo so either could have been the course of the river that was being used in the 13th century BC.

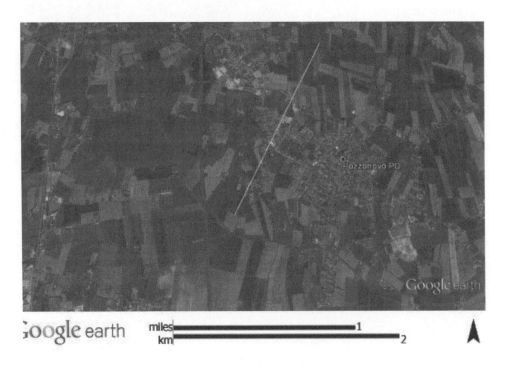

Figure 79 There appear to be features corresponding to older water courses spaced 2 miles apart around the town of Pozzonovo.

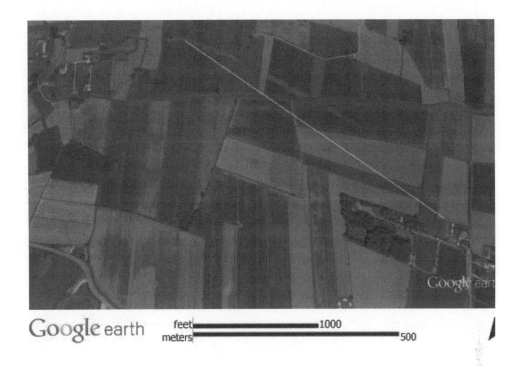

feet ━━━━━━━━━━━━━━ 1000
meters ━━━━━━━━━━━━━━━━━ 500

Figure 80 The feature north of Pozzonovo fits a curve with a radius of around 0.5 to 1 mile so it could potentially be one of the canals around the city

The dialog does refer to stone walls in white, black and yellow (sometimes translated as red) stone. It also refers to towers and gates of stone and coverings of bronze, tin and copper. The acropolis contained the temple of Poseidon which was a stadium long and half as wide but this could mean anything from 300x150 to over 600x300ft. I would guess the first figure would be closer to a real estimate. It was also outlandish in appearance according to the dialog. There may or may not be any remains of these structures if they genuinely existed.

Google earth   feet ▬▬▬▬▬▬▬▬▬▬▬▬ 4000
km ▬▬▬▬▬▬▬▬▬ 1   ▲

Figure 81 South of Pozzonovo there are two features spaced about 3 stade apart which could be old canals at just over a mile from estimated centre of the Atlantean city

While the buildings may have been destroyed evidence of the embankments above the canals are more likely to have survived. I thought it best to look for evidence of circular deposits from human operations in this vicinity which could be extremely old. There are some such traces apparent around the town of Pozzonova. In the first diagram one can clearly evidence of a circular structure extending over half a mile which would have a diameter of around 2 miles from its curvature. This is NE of the town. On the SW side there are again evidences of tracks which could have been part of this same circular work and almost South of the town there are two pairs of these tracks that have respective widths of 200 and 300 feet spaced apart about 1800 feet (3 stadia).   These dimensions are close to those in the dialog but with the canal widths at 100, 200 and 300 feet rather than 1, 2 and 3 stadia. The ratios of the canals might be in the proportions given but the widths as surmised generally much less, but possibly fitting the dialog at certain points.

While at this time we do not have any archaeological remains from the city called Atlantis, we do have considerable amounts from the Terramare culture as well as other Urnfield groups that have given a good understanding of society in Europe at the end of the bronze age to which I believe we should add Plato's written account of this period.

There are claims that the main city lay just beyond the straits of Gibralter near Cadiz. This is a misunderstanding. It is clear from the dialog that a Bronze Age settlement that was part of the confederation existed at this location and formed the furthest part of the state of Atlantis, however this was not the main island or city as it is far too small and does not fit in almost any way the description given in the dialog of the capital city. It is also clearly described in the dialog as being at Gadeira.

An obvious question is what happened to the people after the earthquakes and floods. In general people are quite resilient and it is most likely a large number of the occupants of the Po valley survived the calamities. The dialog talks of the destruction of the Greek cities but obviously the Greeks survived, so I think we can assume the Atlanteans also survived but they were no longer at the centre of trade to the Mediterranean world.

The evidence points to the partial rebuilding of their community, but with the general state of decline and the migrations taking place after this disastrous period it seems likely that the people continued their existence in greatly reduced circumstances. The Villanovians appear and then the Etruscans to fill the vacuum as the iron-age unfolds.

One reason that there is no written history in the Bronze and Iron Age in Europe is that its religious members specialised in memorising and reciting history to an exacting extent. It took a Druid up to 30 years of learning to be fully qualified. We find in ancient Greece long and complex poems such as the Iliad and the Odyssey by Homer. These were originally meant to be read to an audience and in some cases sung. So the verbal tradition was more important than the literal one and so great care was taken in memorising accounts accurately so we can now look at how the rest of the details fit what we know.

Chapter 5

Checking the facts presented

We now need to look into the details of the society that Plato is describing to see how it matches that of the Terramare culture in the Po valley in the LBA and compare this to what we know about the middle to late Bronze Age in Europe.

Figure 82 Reconstruction of bronze-age Lake settlement in Germany

As a starting point it would be useful to estimate how many people occupied the city and the plain surrounding it. As a starting point the dialog gives the dimensions of the city as roughly 2 to 3 miles in diameter

A town of diameter 2 to 3 miles is not particularly large for a capital city and we can estimate its population at about 30,000 plus or minus 10,000. This could be a low estimate for population of the city when comparing it to other cities co-existing at this time such as Mycenae, Knossos or Troy.

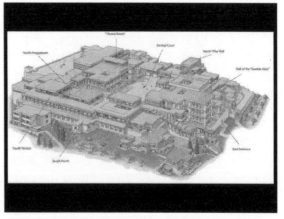

Figure 83 Knossos in Crete and its surrounding area had a population around 100,000 around 1200bc

Estimates for the population size of Mycenae are at around 30,000 and for Knossos higher at around 100,000. So we would expect the size of the capital to be in this region. Cecrops, the mythical founder of Athens is supposed to have carried out a population estimate in around 1500bc and required everyone subject to Athens to bring a stone a deposit it. When counted they totalled 20,000. This probably did not include women or children so the total for the population would be in the ballpark of what we are talking about.

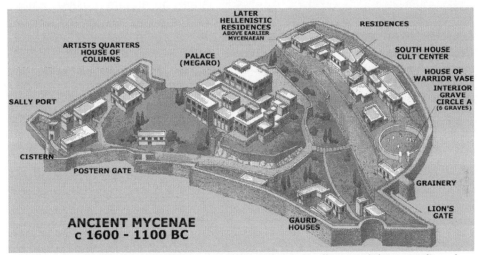

Figure 84 A reconstruction of Mycenae shows the cyclopean walls around the acropolis and shows it was big enough for a large number of people to withdraw into when threatened. The population of the city and surrounding area would have been around 30000.

We can now consider the population of the rest of the plain around the city. The plain is described as being broken into 60,000 parcels of land 10x10 stadia or 100 square stadia in area (3000x2000 stadia being the total area) and on average 3 persons were supplied to meet the military requirements of the region.

The dialog states a sixth part of a list of equipment and personnel had to be supplied from a list which included 18 personnel. So the total size of the military force would have been about 180,000 by this account. If we assumed that between a half and a quarter the men of a fighting age would have been included as a rough guide, as not all could be taken for this purpose even in a dire emergency, then the population estimate would be around 1 to 2 million persons for the region or around 30 persons per square mile.

The population of Egypt in the middle kingdom is estimated at around 2 million in an area of 40,000 square miles. The Po valley is similar in many ways as it is a valley irrigated by large rivers with excellent soil and is slightly larger at around 60,000 square miles. If one assumed a slightly lower population density it seems that 1 to 2 million would fit this comparative model.

Figure 85 Reconstruction of a Terramare house in the plain of the Po valley. These houses could be built in blocks within an enclosure of in smaller numbers throughout the region.

It takes only around 2 acres to support a family and as I stadia is equivalent to 8 acres it would certainly mean that 1 person per stadia would be a safe saturation figure for population density. Whereas, the above parcels on my calculation would represent only a tenth of this density.

Recent astro-archaeological studies of Egypt have identified numerous previously unknown sites dating from the 2nd millennium which suggests population for this period could be considerably lower than actual levels.

Each of the 60,000 divisions would have then totalled about 30 people. Interestingly, it is generally accepted today that 25 or 30 people are the maximum in which personal communication across the levels from the headman to the rest of the group

Figure 86 A reconstruction of what a Terramare house may have looked like inside

is possible. Beyond this level, hierarchies form where personal contact is very limited between the leaders and the populous. The aggregation of 6 of these units to form a community of around 150 to 200 persons would fit with effective models for people management. Beyond this would governmental and ruling hierarchies would operate. The ratio between commoners and nobles including knights during medieval England is around this ratio.

Reconstructions of enclosed settlements confirm populations of around 200 to 300 people. A recently discovered village from the bronze-age near Reading in the UK consisted of identical wattle and daub houses laid out in a regular pattern which was similar to current concepts of mass housing construction leading to be referred to as a Bronze Age Barratt Village. We can safely assume the fact we accidently uncovered one such village in the UK probably means there were large number of them, the traces of which have completely disappeared with time.

Figure 87 This photograph clearly shows the outlines of an abandoned Bronze-age farm in Cornwall with clearly defined field boundaries

Studies have shown that forests were almost completely cleared from the region by the end of the bronze-age and the area would look like a flat plain. Massive amounts of wood were required for the construction of habitations and it appears that this was to such an extent that the area was deforested and there was a shortage of accessible timber, hence the comment in the dialog about '...timber being floated down the rivers'. This would have not been necessary unless the valley had not been deforested. The plain is also referred to as a uniform flat plain which exactly fits the description of this region.

Farmland was laid out with well-defined boundaries by the latter part of the bronze-age.

Figure 88 Example of Bronze age fields in Surrey, such layouts occurred throughout much of Europe with stone walls or fences forming the boundaries

Population densities of around 5 persons per square mile are suggested for Britain during the bronze-age, so a figure of several times this would be expected for this highly fertile valley, which indicates we are in the right ball park and if anything the population would have been higher than a million. So the society we are looking at if very considerable and its military force considerable for the period.

From the above analysis you can see the city was not big for the population. Its population of say 30,000 was small as a percentage compared to say London at 10m in a population of 70m. This was because it was primarily a farming society and not an industrial one.

The dialog says that the island of Atlantis was divided into districts then villages within a district and then leaders of an allotment within a village. There were 60,000 allotments each 10x10 stadia in size. The leader of each allotment had to provide the sixth part of a list which included a war chariot plus two horses and riders plus an additional pair of horses and a charioteer and combatant with a light shield, two hoplites, two archers, two slingers, three stone throwers and three javelin men and four sailors as a part of a complement of 1200 ships.

Taking the last item, this would imply 40 sailors per ship. The Medinet Habu shows ships of the Sea Peoples which would be typical of the time and indeed they have 10 oars each side and two rowers per oar. Interestingly, barges on the Nile had 20 oars each side with an oarsman. The warships would have been shorter to be more manoeuvrable hence the two rowers per oar. The ships would have carried another 80 soldiers or more as outlined in the list above.

Figure 89 Sea battle between Ramses III and the sea peoples shows the sizes of the ships, with roughly two sets of 10 oars making 20 to 40 rowers.

The number of ships given in the list of ships of the Greeks by Homer in the Iliad is also around 1200 ships and around 140,000 men, quite a large army. The contingent represents a loose union of city states ruled by hereditary families with the high king of Mycenae in charge. Homer reckoned there were roughly 10 Achaens to every Trojan householder (meaning Troy has a population around 20 to 30,000). This again confirms the population numbers.

Finally, we know from studies of the Terramare that they grew large amount of cereals and that the region was laid out in fields, so it is hard to conclude that there could not have been anything but a large population inhabiting this valley at this time.

The density of settlements so far found is much less than that estimated above but large areas of the Po valley where densities could have been much higher were flooded after the end of the Terramare and could have buried many sites (Cardelli 1989 and Cremaschi 1991-2).

Terramare crops included: wheat, barley, millet, beans, flax and vines and livestock included cattle, pigs, sheep and goats. Dogs and horses were present. Pottery and metalworking were also established. We can assume that this region created an agricultural surplus which would have been traded for manufactured goods, metal, wood and luxury foods.

We should now consider the nature of the habitations and settlements. Most of the population would have lived in thatched huts. These huts were built on stilts thatched with wattle and daub and built within an enclosure surrounded by running water in which houses were arranged in an orderly fashion, in straight lines with streets crossing at right angles. At Castellazo a rectangular terrace was also present towards the eastern side with possibly a religious purpose. The size of these villages got increasingly larger from the MBA (middle bronze-age) to the RBA with some covering as much as 60ha. Cemeteries were also present where the ashes of the dead were placed in urns and interned as consistent with the Urnfield culture.

Figure 90 Silchester in early iron-age as reconstructed from archaeological evidence gives an idea of what a small village might have looked like in northern Europe

Figure 91 Nuraghe chief with cloak cap, sword and staff of office Sardinia bonze-age.

Such a large population would have been capable of undertaking the kind of works described in the dialog. Society in Europe had undergone considerable changes in the bronze-age with the rise of warrior societies which had spread throughout Europe by the middle of the second millennium. By this time even the dress code had become standardised with a cloak over a tunic, hat and decorative sword indicating warrior status. Odysseus when he was stranded naked on a beach was offered a cloak and tunic then a hat and later a sword to complete his return to his aristocratic status. The tumulus culture which had spread throughout this region reflected the importance of the warriors who were now buried in large tombs covered with substantial mounds. The appearance of razors and combs in burials confirms the increasing importance of appearance in terms of status. With the rise of the warriors, society had changed and religion had less control over societies as secular authority was imposed. The rise of

Figure 92 Gold cap of a warrior Mycenaean

elites led to centralisation of control and to more vertical societies with the tripartite warrior, priestly peasant class model. It is also at this time that the mother goddess is being replaced by the male warrior gods across Europe and the Mediterranean. The cult of the warrior led to the growth of professional armies with full time soldiers and with sophisticated equipment such as

Figure 93 Warriors helmet from Danish Bronze-age

chariots and warships. The warrior elites did not concern themselves with farming and so became distanced from the population they now governed, the

age of the mother goddess and small local agrarian communities had come to an end to be replaced by much larger warlike military societies. Hence Plato's comment on how they had become degenerate in their obsession with power and wealth although their society was at its most prosperous. It is because of the move to such a situation that it was possible for these Kings who had achieved absolute authority to agree to work in a confederation with the objective of enslaving the whole Mediterranean by military conquest. The change in society had roughly been from quasi-democratic societies to oligarchies to possibly tyrannies as mirrored in Plato's Republic.

Figure 94 Copy of clothing Egtved woman was wearing when buried

The excavations of the burial mounds in Denmark of the so called bog peoples led to the discovery of sets of clothing used in the Bronze Age as in the case of the Egtved woman. Men often wore a cloak and a hat. Combs were common and women had complex hairstyles held together with pins. They wore gold jewellery and men had highly crafted swords and daggers which reflected their status in society as did gold table wear. This reflected the new hierarchical nature of the society they now inhabited. These changes were particularly apparent in both religious and burial practices where the old mother goddess and sun worship had been replaced by warrior gods such as Poseidon and Zeus and where burials of chiefs took place in massive tumuli (mounds) giving the name to the Tumulus culture that spread to southern Europe from 1600 to 1300bc. Large tumuli had been built in the UK and elsewhere since the stone-age or more possibly since the arrival of the beaker folk in 2600bc or even earlier. However at this time most internments were family type burials in chambered or passageway tombs associated with the mainly small settlement agrarian based societies that existed before the arrival of the beaker folk traders.

Figure 95 Silbury Hill in Hampshire UK is an excellent example of a tumulus dating from the middle of the 3rd millennium. Whether it contains a grave is unknown, but it occupies a key position on Salisbury plain not far from Stonehenge and many of these mounds contain burials.

Trade now operated over very long distances, examples of this long distance trade includes the Urumchi mummies of the Tarim basin in central Asia which

have been dated to from 2000 to 1000bc and have Caucasian and European DNA markers with intermarriage to far eastern stock a common feature, suggesting links as far as China during the bronze-age. It was also noted that many of the textiles bore a close resemblance to those being produced in Austria vicinity during the bronze-age. It seems likely that trade links were very extensive.

Figure 96 The Mold Cape, possibly acquired by wealth from metal trading made arm movement very difficult and probably was strictly for ceremonial purpose

The appearance of traders bringing metallurgy and long distance contacts and new technologies had led to increased farming production and new industries but the wealth had congregated in the hands of the middle men. The Mold cape is an example of the wealth acquired by metalwork industry owners in the early second millennium. The rise of wealthy elites required them to protect their interests and the hire of enforcers to look after their interests.

Figure 97   The Rock of Monselice still has a fort at its summit that dates from medieval times but there are also traces of occupation during the Bronze Age, which have been uncovered by archaeological investigation. Stone was mined during Roman and subsequent times and a series of embankments can be seen in the diagram above from Monselice Tourist Information.

This rapidly evolved into an oligarchic society, which then became increasing polarised with the smallholders occupying the lower levels. It is likely the priestly class maintained its hold on knowledge and intellect and afforded a way out for members of the underclass who had useful skills but were excluded from the aristocratic elite. In turn the military elite would have recognised the value of the knowledge that the priestly class could supply.

There is no proof that the catastrophe that befell the city and the subsequent climatic change led to the disappearance of the peoples from this region. In fact it seems likely many survived all these events but that their society underwent some radical changes as a result. The Villanovian culture appeared shortly afterwards and then the Etruscans.   The Este culture bridged the gap between the former regime and the new order.   It is certainly likely that a large percentage of the population survived these disasters but would not have been able to rebuild due to the worsened climate and the levels of damage, which would have in any event taken years to resolve, so they would have left to join the general migrations of this difficult time in history greatly reducing the population density.

The main means of travel during the Bronze Age was along rivers or by sea. Travel by land was much riskier and also much slower, so where possible rivers were used as the main method of communication. The major rivers in Europe are the Danube, Rheine, Rhone, Elbe and Vistula which along with their tributaries give excellent coverage. Most major cities are based on rivers and just as roads follow the paths of railways and canals, these in turn often follow rivers and passes that have been in use for thousands of years.

Figure 98 Salzburg links the ore mountains and Lake Konstance and acted as a crossroads for trade in central Europe. The Danube was a major highway linking European regions.

Amber was also highly coveted and extremely valuable and was mainly sourced from the coasts of Denmark and Germany. The amber trade routes criss-crossed Europe during the bronze-age but one important route was from the Adriatic along the Adige as far as Lake Constance where it joins the Rhone and the Rhine.

Originally bronze had been made by amalgamating copper and arsenic but by the middle Bronze-age most bronze was made using tin in a range from 3 to 15 percent but mostly at 10 percent for weapons. The superior strength of this bronze

Figure 99 Salzburg castle sits on a rock outcrop that has been in use antiquity and would have played a similar to that of Montselice in the Bronze-age when the course of the Adige flowed next to it

led to the quest for sources of tin to meet the growing demand.

The reason for this lay in the hardness of the metal which is given in various hardness scales such as the Vickers scale. On this scale tin is very soft at 5HV and copper much harder at 50HV. However bronze can be up to 228HV. As a comparison mild steel is less at 140HV and annealed copper 128HV. So tin became incredibly valuable. There were a number of major sources of tin, which in order of importance were: Cornwall

Figure 100 St Michael's Mount, possibly Ictis in legend was probably a trading post for local tin in the Bronze-age its defensive position would have been its attraction

and Devon in UK, Erzgebirge (Ore Mountains) in Germany, Brittany in France and the Iberian Peninsula in Spain.

Salzburg, which is close to Lake Konstance was the ancient centre of Chalcopyrite copper production at places such as Mittenburg. The bronze procured was of much better quality than that which used Grey Copper Ore, but the fact that this replaced the use of Chacopyrite, around 1200-1100bc, indicates that either it was inaccessible or unavailable after this time.

The Ore Mountains lie roughly halfway between the Adriatic and the Baltic and about 50km north of Salzburg. Their discovery led to the growth of the Unetice culture, which by the MBA had become the dominant and richest social group in Western Europe.

Figure 101 Mont St Michel in Brittany was also probably a tin trading post in the bronze-age and part of the system connecting tin trade along the north Atlantic coast

The amber trade route from Denmark stated at the mouth of the Elbe just north west of Hamburg and continued along the Elbe to Magdeburg then Dresden and on to Prague where it is now named the Vltaya. Today cruise ships sail all the way from Hamburg to Prague along the Elbe which demonstrates how useful a route this river has always provided to reach the central regions of Europe from the North Sea. The Vltaya continues south until it reaches a lake within a few miles west of Linz through which the Danube flows. The Danube not only connects to Salzburg and Budapest but stretches from the Black Sea as far as the where the three rivers, Danube, Rhone and Rhine virtually join around Basel and Lake Neuchatel. North of Salzburg a branch of the Danube continues to Innsbruck and the Brenner Pass continues on into Italy to join the Adige and enter the Po valley.

Figure 102 Elbe river flows from the north sea far south into the alps coming within a few miles of the Danube

The route north along the Adige River which became extinct around 100bc due to an avulsion, was more important than along the current river referred to as the Po as it allowed access far into central Europe. The Alps to the west are far too high to be easily passable. This route was recalled in Apollonius of Rhodes 'Voyage of the Argo' where Jason is forced to sail up the Eridanus as far as it goes to a lake where it meets the Rhone down which he continues back to the Mediterranean. He refers to the Amber Isles at the end of the Chronian Sea. And the innermost blessed amber isle. He also refers to the stench in the air.

In the dialog it refers to the ten kingdoms which formed an alliance and held sway over numerous other islands within the Mediterranean and outside in the Atlantic Ocean. In specific it controlled Libya up to the borders of Egypt and

Europe as far as Tyrrhenia. The kingdom on the furthest part of the island was by the Pillars of Heracles and faced Gadeira.

As already discussed, the Bronze Age structures of the Nuraghe in Sardinia are very closely linked with those in the Balearic Islands (Majorca was home to the Talayot Culture who built cyclopean structures such as the Navetas and Taula shrines) and also to those in Sicily. There are also similarities with the Almerian culture of the same time and the Castellera of the Istrian peninsula east of the Venetian plain. These islands probably needed to be highly fortified as they

Figure 103 The Ringen Roysa from a Bronze age burial site in Avaldsnes in Norway shows a stone copy of the worldly home of the deceased with a boat ready to take the deceased's soul to the otherworld.

could have been easy prey to pirates. However, the field systems in Britain and also in the Terramare indicate that they did not need such large defences and that they were relatively less worried by attack. This may be due to the fact that they were much militarily stronger than these islands and so less threatened. There are in fact many references to the piracy in the west of the Mediterranean at this time.

The rings of land and water around the city of Atlantis were probably originally defensive but may also been connected with a belief system. A very similar design was uncovered under a burial mound in Norway where stone monument which depicted three alternate bands of water and land which surround the tomb with a ship placed to leave, presumably to carry the soul with goods to the otherworld.

Figure 104 The citadel at Buda overlooking the Danube in Budapest. This hill was occupied far back into prehistory and would have been on one of the trade routes in use in the middle and late bronze-age.

It is quite clear from literature closer to the time that the Greeks believed the amber isles lay at the top of the Adriatic Sea, but they also believed that the amber came from islands straight beyond the Pillars of Heracles. So they would have assumed that these islands were in the same place and accessible from both the Adriatic and up along the Atlantic Ocean outside the straights.

 The Atlantic was known as the Sea of Atlas and the Adriatic as the Chronian Sea as, interestingly, was the ice bound sea far in the North. This suggests they saw a connection between the Adriatic Sea accessed from the North Sea and maybe the Baltic and the Adriatic. It is possible they had no access to the English Channel and the taking a route through the Irish Sea or into the Atlantic would have brought sailors into seas so rough that it would have deterred then from further progress.

The Atlantic is actually referred to as the Sea of Atlas in the original Greek version and the passage in Greek reads '... impassable to the sea beyond ' rather than Atlantic. The translation varies according to the translator. So the exact descriptions are not totally reliable

Greek writers noted that they had forgotten how they had founded the city at Sais in antiquity. After the fall of Troy it is recorded that the Greeks wandered the Mediterranean. Odysseus is one example. Many of the Greeks were not received back favourably according to legend. The records at Medinet Habu record the attacks of the sea peoples which took place roughly from 1250 to 1160bc. At first they appear to have been simply raiding but later seeking a new place to settle. The chronology of the dialog place the founding of Sais at around 1250bc plus-minus 50 years – so this is about right. The Sea Peoples were a confederation, who were dispossessed and their origin in the Adriatic would be one possibility. The main candidates include the Atlanteans, Trojans

Figure 105 Amber is washed up on the beaches along the Baltic and north European coasts and is particularly easy to find in Denmark.

and Greeks with various allies. In general I would favour the Greeks as the Trojans were not actually completely defeated. They retreated inland after

Troy was sacked but returned, if they left it would have more likely been due to the period of drought rather than for conquest reasons. The Greeks forces were actually in a worse position. They had been away for well in excess of 10 years and people at home had moved on. So their return was not particularly welcomed, particularly as harvests may have been bad. The drought had caused real problems for the Terramare and it is possible again that pressures caused by reduction in the population carrying capacity of the region had led to foraging expeditions rather than abandonment.

One question is why the northern Adriatic would have made the best route for trade to the Mediterranean world. The western Mediterranean may have been relatively lawless and subject to piracy according to many accounts. This is certainly the case at the time on the Minoan empire.

The annexing of the islands and regions such as Tyrrhenia could well have been to protect their trading interests and to expand them, just for the same reasons as the Mycenaeans attacked Troy.

The route through ports on the black sea would have served the Hittite and Assyrian empire, but may have been more problematic than the route through the Adriatic before the rise of Mycenae

The northern Adriatic was certainly the closest port for access to the industrial German heartland directly north and also for the amber and tin from northern Europe. Much of this may have been converted into bronze in the Carpathian basin and southern Germany before being moved on for processing into goods in the Mediterranean.

The Castelleria at places such as Monkodonja near Rovigno in Istria were large walled settlements with an acropolis and palace in the centre surrounded by residential buildings. They are dated from 1800 to 1200bc, when they were abandoned. They had zig-zag entrances and a deep cave adjoined suggesting a religious aspect to the site as well. Istria is famous for its durable pure white limestone which has been extensively used in many Italian cities such as Venice. Many churches in Italy feature the use of alternate white Istrian stone and Red Veronese Brocatello stone giving their distinctive red and white pattern. The dialogue refers specifically to red, white and black stone which fits with these sources of stone. The forts in Istria are estimated at over 350, most of which are in very poor state and have not been excavated. It is however quite clear that just like Sardinia, Istria was heavily fortified during the Bronze-age. Forts such as these were common in Europe in the Bronze Age.

Hill forts appeared in Europe around the 16th century bc. They were built on small hills and often featured defensive banks and ditches. Good examples are at Hueneburg just north of Lake Constance and close to Matrei on the Brenner Pass near Innsbruck. The topographical map of Monselice Rock suggest it may have also been an early Bronze Age hillfort and the description of alternating defensive rings of embankment and ditch in Plato's dialogue closely fits this. In fact there appear to be three distinct embankments clearly visible today.

It appears from recent archaeology that central Europe had become far more integrated by the late bronze-age than has been previously thought, and the idea that a confederation to sort out trade issues would have arisen seems quite logical as it would have been obvious that working together to maximise trade was in everyone's interest . These islands would have been independent but convened, just as we do today, to try to resolve a common approach to commerce based around mutual self-interest.

As to what became of the Atlanteans, Cato the Elder recalled the Eugenei which means well born as an ancient and once powerful people and referred to them in his lost work Origines. He counted them among the major tribes of antiquity, he was still able to numerate 34 towns they had possessed and that they were reported by tradition to have once occupied all the land between the Alps and the Adriatic Sea . Pliny the Elder also claimed they were driven by the Venetii at the start of the 1st millennium to the Adige, Lake Como area and that the Stoni tribe of Trentino were the same people. They were collectively later referred to as Ligurians, who are widely acknowledged as one of the major tribes of ancient Europe. The Venetii were immigrants after the fall of Troy according to Myth and seized the lands in the North Adriatic by force.

In conclusion the facts given in the dialog match almost completely with what we know about the inhabitants of the North Adriatic and of Europe at the time of the events recorded by Plato in his dialogues.

Chapter 6

Myth and religion

In this chapter I will first look at the Greek mythology and religion to see how it

fits with the dialog and then at that of northern Italy and Europe.

One wonders why when so many names and acts were remembered in literature including myths and poetry by the Greeks that this, their greatest achievement, was not. The answer may be that it was because it was deliberately buried as it caused a problem with the religious orders of the time and would have compromised their authority and so mention of it would have been a heresy. If this war had been undertaken by Zeus and others then he was clearly a mortal historical figure rather than a god

The Romans were also very severe to anyone who questioned the authority of their Gods. Many early Christians were executed for refusing to accept their divinity. This is despite the fact

Figure 106 A statue of Zeus in his typical pose holding a thunderbolt in his right hand.

that Livy and others clearly thought much of their religion was ridiculous.

The reality was that no matter what the Roman establishment actually thought about their religion, they were ruthless in imposing its authority on the masses as it was an important means of control that they understood kept order over the majority. Likewise the Greek establishment perceived it the same way. So the story of the war with the Atlanteans was changed into a war between Gods and the original versions of the events were presumably obfuscated.

The ending of Critias is strange. The first sentence would seem to be the appropriate ending for the previous section. I wonder if it breaks off because Plato knew that this story was potentially about the gods and that although he had argued strongly for good gods he refuted any ideas of the mortal nature of gods (such as the story of Leda , where Zeus turns himself into a swan, as he argued god would not do such a thing). Socrates was accused firstly for trying to teach new gods and then when that was difficult to prove, not believing in any gods and condemned to death for impiety. So, Plato had to steer a very careful course between evolving his ideas and avoiding upsetting the religious establishment. The death of Socrates had

Figure 107 *The Erecthion on the acropolis at Athens. This is a replacement of an earlier one destroyed in the Persian war.*

played heavily on him. He was well aware that clever philosophers were not generally popular with the masses and they would be aggressive to anything that challenged their accepted beliefs.

The dialog explains in several places that due to the catastrophes that befell Athens that literacy had been almost lost and only the names of the rulers but little of their achievements were passed down. Later in the same text it says '... that is how the names but not the achievements of these early generations come to be preserved '. It is therefore not surprising that complex historical events became simplified and distorted for mass consumption.

The priests at Sais told Solon that their (Greek) myths were in fact Genealogies, if we take this as true, then it they can become a very useful tool when coupled with archaeological evidence in building a picture of the past. It is worth remembering that much of the Iliad consists of lists which are meaningless to us but could have been very significant to listeners at the time who would have identified with them. It is also important to get inside the mind of the Greeks. When Homer says the a god or goddess such as Aphrodite was at the battle but was injured and then recovered by the following day to lead them back into battle, he is referring to effigies that were carried (just as Crusaders carried a cross in front of them and until recently we carried flags) for good luck. If such an effigy was damaged it would be bad luck, but then of course it would be back the following day repaired and looking better probably than before. So, the text is in fact accurate in its description, it is just the way we read it that seems to make it appear a fabrication. The same of course applies to Myths, they contain elements of historical fact intermixed with symbolic content. Whereas the original listeners would have clearly understood the symbolism, much of it is lost to us.

Figure 108 *The bronze-age city of Tiryns may have acted as a strategic stronghold for the Mycenaean empire. It was destroyed around 1200bc*

Plato in the dialog goes on to say that Cecrops, Erectheus, Ericthonious and Erusichthon were mentioned in the text. We know little of Cecrops other than him being a mythical king of Athens. But Erectheus was highly acclaimed and a large monument to him was erected on the Acropolis in Athens, the Erectheum. Myths recall that he won a war against Eleusis and the Thracians and named Cecrops his son as his successor and this was most likely a real event as it was remembered up into Hellenistic times and celebrated annually. According to the mythical chronology of St Jerome, Erectheus became king of Athens at around 1350bc and Cecrops around 1330bc. His father was Ericthonious, hence, the reference to genealogies by the priests at Sais. Cecrops was a contemporary of Zeus according to legend and the first king to acknowledge Zeus as a god. The first Cecrops who was recorded as a king of Athens was claimed to have introduced the Zeus cult in around 1480bc according to various accounts. Some sources believe that Erectheus and Erichthonius were one and the same and it cannot be proved one way or the other.

We know from numerous myths that Heracles and Telamon were contemporaries and that after Heracles sacked Troy, that one surviving royal child was Priam, king of Troy and father of Helen. This puts the sacking by Heracles at around 1300bc. We also told that Priam's father was Laomedon and his father Ilus who built Ilium and in turn his father was Tros. Laomedon's uncle was Ganymede, whom Zeus abducted, and in exchange for Ganymede Zeus gave Thos horses, so again they were contemporaries. This places Zeus and Tros as being alive around 1350bc. We also know from Strabo and other sources that Cecrops was the first king to acknowledge Zeus as a god.

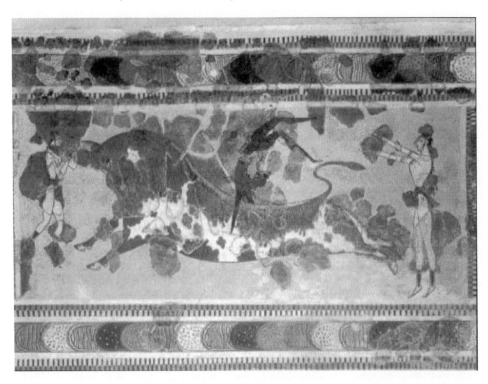

Figure 109 The famous wall painting from Knossos showing the bull leapers in action. The Cretians were bull worshippers in the bronze-age and this may have been a test of courage.

The war that took place between Athens and Atlantis took place around 1350bc and we know that Erectheus had achieved a great victory over Eleusis and the Thracians at around 1350bc. Erectheus defeated the Elusian army under Eumopolis, their king but formerly a Thracian prince, and killed him. Erectheus himself was later killed by Poseidon, being struck down by his trident for killing his son Eumopolis. These dates fit the time for the war referred to in the dialogue and Thrace was under control of the Atlanteans.

After Erectheus , the people of Athens chose Athena over Poseidon as their main god and from the dialog on Atlantis we know that the Atlanteans were followers of Poseidon. Athens then took control of Eleusis. We know from finds by the acropolis that Athens withstood a major siege during the 13th century bc which supports the mythical account of events at this time.

The dialog in Timaeus states that at the time of the war with Atlantis that Athens was pre-eminent in war and conspicuously the best governed in every way, its achievements being and constitution being the finest of any in the world of which we have heard tell.

Figure 110 Theseus slaying the Minotaur. This shows the assertion of Athens over Knossos as well as the rejection of bull worship by the Athenians.

We refer to this period in Greek history as the empire of the Mycenaeans. However, there is no evidence that Mycenae was the centre of such an empire other than that it led the Greeks in the Trojan War at a much later date. The historical records that we possess tell a very different story. The historical record gives Perseus as the founder of Mycenae, at a later date. It was not until the archaeological digs that Mycenae took on its present status. Part of the reason was Mycenae had been abandoned and therefore there was much to be found, whereas Athens has been continuously occupied and any remains from the Bronze Age have either been destroyed or are buried under later structures, so we have little evidence from this period to go on.

We have numerous sources for the genealogies of the archaic kings. One particularly good record is the Parian Chronicle dating from several centuries BC and currently thought to have relied on historical records held at Athens. This stela was found in the 18th century on the island of Paros and listed kings and events back into antiquity.

The written histories give the earliest king of Athens as being Cecrops. He was succeeded by Amphyction who had married his daughter. Cecrops came from Egypt according to legend and brought a framework for social organisation with him. He introduced laws such as marriage and an organised legal system and established the Areopagus. Cecrops was succeeded by Cranaus who continued the process. He was succeeded by Amphyction who realised that uniting the local villages together in an alliance would enable them to combat incursions of raiding parties

Figure 111 An Hellenistic statue of Atlas holding the world on his shoulders as punishment for fighting against in the battle of the gods and titans.

from sea and land. He formed the Amphyctrionic League. After Amphyction the next kings were Ericthonious, Pandion and then Erectheus. He introduced the cult of Demeter (Ceres) and fought Eleusis in a war which the Athenians won. His general was Ion, son of Xuthus who was a son of Deucalion. It was either Erectheus or Ion who introduced the four part system of class divisions, labourers, artisans, priests and military. In the dialog in Timaeus the priest s tell Solon 'First our priestly class is kept distinct from the others, as also is our artisan class , next each class of craftsmen – shepherds, farmers, hunters – performs its function in isolation from others. And you will have noticed our soldier class is kept separate from all others..'.

Figure112 *A statue of Resheph from Gebal, he is a Phoenecian deity but also worshipped in Egypt and wears the crown of upper Egypt, he is the same as Apollo and Poseidon as a sun god.*

According to myth the founder of the Greeks was a person called Danaus who arrived with his daughters from Libya according to legend. The name for the ancient Greeks was the Danaans. We have legends such as those in Ireland of the Tuatha de Danaan or the peoples of Greece. According to their legends these people left Ireland for Greece where they stayed for many years and then returned to Ireland. Other sources claim Danaus came from Egypt. However, many of these myths do seem to record a time around that of Cecrops or just before when Greece was being colonised from abroad. Analysis of settlement sites also suggests that many of these incursions came from the East as this was occupied earlier than many sites in the West.

Most accounts of these colonisers arriving from the east, Egypt, Levant etc. records them bringing social change with them, this includes Danaus, Cecrops, Kadmos among others. It seems reasonable that this may well have happened. The Egyptians themselves were not seafaring, but they ruled over a large area including the Levant, which had many seafaring people among them. So whether they were called Egyptians but in fact Phoenicians, the upshot is the same. Settlers from the sea probably did come from the east bringing change with them and setting up colonies. At the same time the Atlantean successors to the Bell Beaker people were also engaged in colonisation. The Minoans kept some sort of regional control on trade which may have kept a balance until a power vacuum occurred and brought the two colonising powers into direct conflict, a clash between the East and the West.

Figure 113 Wall painting from Akotiri in Santorini, dated around 1600bc at the time of the eruption of Thera. It shows the high level of development of Cretian society at that time and their heavy involvement in trade by sea.

So Athens could have led a confederation as it had a complex well run society with alliances with neighbouring states at the times we are interested in. These alliances did not prevent competition between the states but enabled them to come together to deal with outside threats and placed limits on extents of the internal conflicts that arose by mutual agreement.

Figure 114   The Dupljaja chariot from the eastern European bronze-age shows a sun god (Apollo or Poseidon) in his chariot being pulled by birds.   The cup marks all appear on megalithic monuments such as stone henges throughout Europe as do spiral and other motifs.

Further evidence inlcudes a double joined temple on the acropolis at Athens (which was destroyed by the Persians c480bc) to Cecrops, Erectheus, Athena and Poseidon. There was also a temple to Erectheus and every year up into Hellenistic times, the priests of the Erectheum and the priestesses of Athena would take a precession to Skiron for the Skiron Festival remembering this time. On the pediment of the Parthenon is a carving showing Athens defeating Poseidon. This shows how important the achievements of Erectheus were considered. However, by classical times the actual history of events had been forgotten and replaced with myths. Greek poets wrote plays to explain the reason behind some of the ceremonies that were performed as many Athenians had little knowledge of the origin of the events behind these ceremonies. It may well be that the importance of the war with Eleusis had been forgotten in the mists of time.

There are the remains of a Mycenaean style palace under the acropolis which was dated to around 1300 to 1400bc and very similar to that at Mycenae with cyclopean walls and fortifications. It would be reasonable to assume that Cecrops was the first ruler who was part of the Mycenaean confederacy and as part of this adopted the cult of Zeus. These ties with the other major Mycenaean communities remained strong, although there were times when the member states were at considerable differences, such as when Theseus slew the Minotaur.

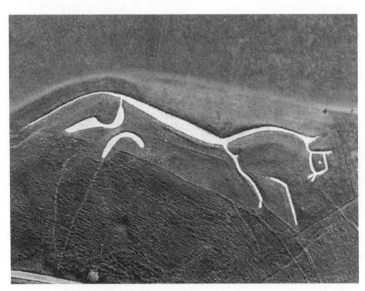

The Athenians had played a very small part in the Trojan War, even though they had sent some ships, they are barely mentioned in the Iliad. There are several possible reasons for this, but a very likely one would be that Theseus had taken Athens on its own course and away from

Figure 115 The Uffington white horse is an example of the cult of horse worship which dates back as far as the arrival of the corded ware people from eastern Europe in the 3rd millennium bc.

being a part of the Mycenaean confederation. The conflict with Minos, King of Crete had arisen when as son of Minos had been assassinated while attending games at Athens. The Athenians agreed to give several of their children every year to Minos in recompense of this act. What became of the children is unclear, legend says they were fed to the Minotaur, but the reality was probably far different. After a while the Athenians came to resent the agreement and wanted to bring it to an end. According to myths, Theseus, who had achieved many feats similar to Heracles in some ways, took up the task. He went with the children to Crete and slew the Minotaur in the Labyrinth. From what we now know, it would appear the Minotaur was either the King or a High Priest, probably wearing the skull of a bull during religious ceremonies performed in the Labyrinth. Many peoples at this time were bull worshippers, so this was not unusual and the wearing of a bull's skull during ceremonies was a feature in Britain in ancient times as well (from bulls skulls found near megalithic sites which had been adapted for wearing).

The real achievement of Theseus, when he became King of Athens was to extend its sphere of influence and for Synoecism (from synokismos in Greek) which means living together, in Attica. The slaying of the Minotaur indicates that Theseus freed Athens from the interference of Crete

Figure 116 A replica of Jason's boat the Argo which he sailed from Argos in his mission to acquire the legendary Golden Fleece. This journey took place period of social collapse

and by doing so lifted the status of Athens accordingly.

So, the monks at Sais told Solon that before the Trojan War, the Athenians had led an alliance and then fought by themselves and routed a considerable power, which he knew little of other than child-like myths.

We are all familiar with the legend that Cronus swallowed his sons and that Zeus was hidden in Crete and a stone offered up instead and that when Zeus grew up he caused Cronus to regurgitate all the sons and that Zeus forced him back into the sea beyond along with the Titans.

According to mythology Zeus was either born on Mount Lykaion or in Crete near Mount Ida. He was a descendant of Uranus, the oldest god. He had fathered many children including the Titans and lastly Cronus. Cronus had married Rhea against advice that his children would usurp him when they were grown. He swallowed them as soon as they were born but rhea hid Zeus and placed a stone in his place. She hid Zeus in a cave in Crete, variously called the Dictyan cave among various names, which was near to Lato in Crete.

Figure 117 The Dikteon cave in Crete is where Zeus is claimed to have been born and hidden as a stone , so avoiding being swallowed by Cronus, his father.

When Zeus reached manhood he got Cronus drunk and forced him to regurgitate his brothers and sister. Zeus then formed an alliance with some of the Titans and fought Cronus in a war that allegedly lasted 10 years. Atlas was the commander of the Titans who did not support Zeus. Zeus won and exiled Cronus and his allies to Tartarus (possibly Sicily) or Elysia. Later the Titans tried to regain their lost power and the battle of the giants and the gods took place, they lost this battle again and Atlas was forced to carry the world on his shoulders Prometheus was expelled into the black sea and chained to a rock.. After this the Ogygian flood occurred. Danaus left Egypt and Cecrops settled in Athens. He allegedly brought the worship of Neith from Sais and this deity later became Athena.

The idea that myths were based on real events was popular even in antiquity, Euhemerus believed Zeus was originally a king of Crete and had died and was buried in Crete and likewise the islanders claimed to have a grave. Like the name Pharaoh and Minos (which means king in the Cretan language of this period) Zeus could also have been a title given to the king when he was made a god, so several people could have held that same name. The acts of cult followers of Zeus could also have been attributed to him, as in the case of Hercules and the Heracleidae. So Zeus could have first liberated Crete before either he or his later followers moved on to liberate other colonies.

It is possible that like Minos, Zeus was a title held by the King. The Heracles we think of in Greek myths was in fact called Alcaeus but his name was changed to the Egyptian god Heracles (who was far more ancient) as his stature increased.

There are also records of more than one Zeus. There is the Zeus born in the Dictean cave who was a son of Uranus and a brother of Atlas and the Olympian Zeus who was a son of Cronus but fought him. This rather suggests a cult around a real person that had more than one centre. The Olympian Zeus was the later and more famous one that defeated Cronus and the titans. Suggesting the events in Crete concerning Zeus, preceded those in Attica in Greece.

Figure 118 The Egyptian goddess Neith shown with her symbols of office around her including the red crown of lower Egypt Her worship may have been brought to Athens by Cecrops

From the labours of Heracles it is obvious he was not part of the ruling elite in the earlier part of his life, but was later raised to being a God (or rather a demi-god).

Sanchuniathon of Berytus (Beirut) is believed to have lived before the Trojan War. He claimed his writings came from inscriptions in Phoenecian temples, which exposed the truth that the gods were originally humans who came to be worshipped as gods and that the Phoenicians had taken the names of kings and applied them to elements of the Cosmos. It has also been claimed that Philo forged this work, however much of what he said has been supported by Ugaric texts uncovered at Ras Sharma since 1929. We know the Phoenicians worshipped both Apollo and Poseidon.

So possibly the war with Atlantis was remembered in myth as the war waged by a Zeus against a Cronus of which the war with Eleusis had been a part. This would account for why the greatest achievement of the Greeks had been forgotten, as it would have created a conflict with the doctrine of the cult of Zeus which ruled the Greek world at that time.

This feat by Zeus made him a god. So let us suppose what the Olympian Zeus and his followers actually did was to build the confederation referred to in the dialog by liberating and assimilating various colonies formerly taken over by the Titans under Cronus. It has been common for great leaders to be made into gods and for cults to follow on from them, even up until Roman times when the Emperor Augustus was made a god along with his successors.

Figure 119 A Hellenistic statue of Icarus

The story of Daedalus may well be closely related to the war referred to in the dialog. According to various sources, Daedalus was a great inventor who came to be employed by Minos, King of Crete. He built the labyrinth in which Minos hid the Minotaur. When Daedalus threatened to leave, Minos imprisoned him and his son Icarus.

However Daedalus invented wings, or in actual reality more likely sails, from

Figure 120 The Strettweg Chariot from Graz Museum is a cult object dating from the Urfield Culture. It depicts a ceremony presided over by a female deity

feathers which were held together with wax. Daedalus and his son escaped and outran the pursuing Minoans. Icarus had been warned not to sail to close to the sun, however he ignored this advice and as a result fell and was drowned (his boat capsized). Daedalus escaped to Sicily and sought refuge with the King, who granted him safety. Minos set off with a great fleet to find Daedalus and learned through a clever trick that he was in Sicily. However Daedalus contrived the death of Minos and the Sicilians as a result destroyed the fleet of the Minoans (burned according to Herodotus). The Minoans never recovered and they were subject to attacks from the Sicilians and the Sardinians (according to Polybius). Allegedly, Zeus regained control of Crete and expelled the invaders. Minos was buried in Kamikos in Sicily but later re-interned in Crete. We know the empire of the Minoans came to an end around 1420 to 1375bc. Many historians believe the story of Daedalus has an historical basis. The Sicilians and Sardinians would have been part of the confederacy of Atlantis, so here we have another version of the Chronians swallowing their offspring or rather the Atlanteans who are one and the same thing as the Chronians taking control of the Crete and presumably other islands before being expelled the followers of Zeus.

Diodorus Sicula refers to the Atlanteans in his books the Library of History. He said they had possessed great cities and formed a pact with the Gorgons who lived in the west. Medusa was queen of the Gorgons and was slain by Perseus, King of Mycenae. Perseus was also a son of Zeus. Heracles finally wiped out the Gorgons when he visited these areas to set up his pillars, this being a reference to the Heracleids, late Bronze Age followers of Hercules who post-date the Trojan War.

Figure 121 The Abbotts Bromley horn dance like Morris dancing is a memory of very ancient rituals still continued into the modern era

According to Diodorus, Atlas was the first to understand the stars and the secret of the sphere, possibly suggesting the Atlanteans had a greater knowledge of the larger world and of astronomy than the Greeks before Heracles.

We are not aware of any written records of these events that still exist today, but many have been lost in antiquity so this may not be surprising. What is strange is that Egypt almost always recorded victories over its enemies and it is hard to find a time when Egypt was the underdog. However one such record does exist which shows Egyptians being held prisoner by Libyan warriors. This is a very strange image to record, but not necessarily when one remembers that 1350 is the date at which Akenhaten became Pharaoh with his queen Nefertiti. He reigned for about 17 years and after his death all records of his reign were obliterated. He withdrew Egypt in on itself and as he became obsessed with building his capital at Amarna. While records such as those of the Amarna records have been found almost all other records have been lost. The Hittites invaded Egyptian territory around this time and were surprised to be unopposed and it is assumed that internal religious upheavals, which were focusing efforts elsewhere, were the cause of this failure to protect their dominions.

Remnants of court records made during the reign of Akenhaten's father, Amenhotep III refer to a number of Cretian cities such as Knossos, Phaestos, Kydonia and Amnisos and do not record any distinction between them. This suggests that at his time these were city states and that Knossos was not pre-eminent. The rise of Knossos may have occurred during the Mycenaean period, but as Minos simply means King in Cretian at this time, it is impossible to know which Minos is actually being referred to in many myths. It does, however, indicate the importance of the trade relationship with Crete at this time and if Crete had been seriously defeated after this period during

Figure 122   Raising the Maypole in Bad Rechenhall, a ceremony that still takes place in many towns across Europe and dates back to before the bronze-age.

Akenhaten's reign, this would have been a matter of great concern to the Egyptians.

Records also show that Amenhotep III who ruled Egypt from 1388 to 1350bc and was the father of Akenhaten fought off attacks by the Libyan's and was accompanied by his son, Akenhaten. During his reign the Sardana also attacked Egypt and piracy by the Lukka people on Cyprus and Syria is also mentioned. This indicates that the Atlanteans, of whom the Sardinians would have been a colony were in an expansionist phase at this time.

129

Figure 123 A pottery depicting Odysseus blinding the Cyclopes. Hellenistic period c.6cent bc

An inscription by Amenhotep son of Hapu who was an official under Amenhotep III refers to the need to secure the Nile delta against a seaborne threat and in a stela dated to the time of Ramses II, known as the Tanis stela because of where it was found we hear of 'the Sherden of rebellious mind, whom none could withstand, they sailed in warships from the middle of the sea'. We also hear how Ramses II 'has destroyed the warriors of the great green sea so lower Egypt can spend the night sleeping peacefully'. This inscription is dated to roughly 1277bc.

The war with the Atlanteans and their allies was probably a long and protracted affair and the event the dialog is concerned with is the Athenian victory that turned the tide may well be remembered as the war with Eleusis and its follow on.

In Greek mythology the flood of Ogygia , which covered the whole world , followed the battle of the gods and giants. Ogygia was an island according to legend. Homer places it near the navel of the sea where the daughter of Atlas lived. Aristotle wrote the Ogygia lay outside the pillars of Heracles where the sea is shallow owing to much mud, but calm as it lies in a hollow. Plutarch states that Ogygia lies 5000 stadia from Britain. In the Odyssey by Homer, Odysseus was held by Calypso on the island of Ogygia for seven years. He eventually was allowed to leave after Hermes, the Giant Slayer visited Calypso when Poseidon was in Ethiopia to warn her to let Odysseus go free. He built a raft and sailed for 20 days. Calypso told him that when he reached Scheria he would be able to get a boat to Ithaca. Sheria was the home of the Phaeacians, a race who had been neighbours to the domineering Cyclopes (a large people) and decided to leave their homes and resettle in Scheria . Poseidon however was on his way back from Ethiopia and caught sight of Odysseus and harried him. However, Ino the daughter of Cadmus (who had finally settled in Illyria) helped him and he made it to Scheria. He had originally arrived in Ogygia after sailing 9 days from the whirlpools of Charbadis and Scylla. He mistook Scheria for Ithaca on his way back as they were close together on the western side of Greece. The most likely location for Ogygia is in the Adriatic, how far up it is difficult to guess but clearly Odysseus was held against his will as Poseidon the earthshaker had kept him in exile though stopped short of killing according to Homer. Finally according to Greek legend Atlantis was the name for Ogygia as it belonged to Leto the daughter of Atlas.

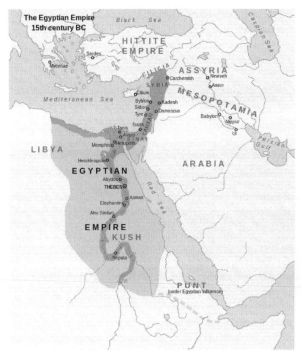

The dialogue says that the Priests told Solon that they both worshipped the same goddess as they had been related to each other in some way in the distant past there society being founded a 1000year (80 solar years give or take plus or minus 40 years for as numbers of years is an approximate figure) later than the Greeks.

In the Odyssey, we learn that Odysseus claimed he had made nine successful raids on foreign lands before the Trojan War. He claimed that his men laid waste the fields of Egypt , killing the men and carrying off women and

Figure 124 The Egyptian empire had spread far up the Levant by the 15th century after the expulsion of the Hyksos and the conquests of the 16th dynasty Pharaohs

children before the Egyptian army arrived and either killed or captured a large number of his men, he himself was held prisoner and spent 5 years in Egypt, during which period – it is claimed – he amassed a fortune. These raids closely resemble those of the Sea Peoples who raided the Egyptian delta from around 1250 to 1150bc. The constitution of the city at Sais was 1000 years later than that of Athens or around roughly 1250bc , which is about same time as the

Greeks started to invade and settle in the Nile delta and the time at which the cult of Neith was adopted in Sais according to the dialogue .

However, it is clear that foreigners had occupied the Nile delta as far back as 1800bc. The Hyksos invaded the delta and shortly afterwards conquered the rest of Egypt and established themselves as Pharaohs around 1650bc as the 15th dynasty. They were expelled by Pharaoh Amhose in around 1550bc. The Hyksos were horse worshippers and brought advances to Egypt such as chariots that greatly impacted the future of Egypt leading to the building of the Egyptian empire. It was during this period that colonisations took place and that the tablets Jason was given much later in Colchis showed how far the Egyptians had explored.

Following the climatic disasters of the 11th century, exploration resumed and Jason set out on his voyage of discovery from Argos. The voyage of the Argo is a sort of guided tour of the trade routes around the end of the first millennium. After the Trojan War, access to the Hellespont had become possible for the Greeks and so an expedition was made with the objective to

Figure 125 The voyage of the Argo took Jason into the Black Sea as far as Colchis and then back up the Danube and into the Adriatic. He would have continued up the Po which he referred to as the Eridanus before returning to Greece via a diversion to the coast near modern day Libya

discover more about the remote regions of the world, in particular the Black Sea and the source of gold and other metals that were arriving from these places.

The Golden Fleece records the discovery made that fleeces were used to recover gold particles from rivers in Colchia (as done here until recent times), located at the Eastern end of the Black Sea in the Caucasian mountains.

The outward journey took them through the straits into the Black Sea and along its southern shore close to modern day Turkey and on to Colchia.

They returned on a more northerly route and ended up either at the delta of the Ister or more probably the Danube, located on the western shores of the Black Sea. There is general agreement that they entered the northern Adriatic, going south and returning to venture up the Po continuing to a lake which could be Lake Constance to then head south along the Rhone to return to the Mediterranean heading south through the Tyrrhenian sea , finally returning to Argos via a tortuous route. The Po no longer gave direct access to the Adige.

This journey took place after the mythical Phaeton had crashed into the Eridanus and refers to the stench arising from the area, this could easily have been marsh gas but as previously mentioned is more likely hydrogen sulphide from mud volcanoes and hot water springs.

Among the next great explorers was Pytheas of Massalia whose journey up the Atlantic and possibly as far as Iceland was recorded by Erastothenes in a lost

work, which has been handed down in poetic form by the Roman poet Rufus Festus Avienus. Himilco, a Carthaginian was another such explorer and from these records it is clear that little was known about the geography of Europe even into Roman times.

One sea change that occurred in society in the Bronze Age was the change in religious worship as gods took on a more human form replacing the part animal human (anthropomorphic) forms which had formerly been associated with much of the Bronze Age pantheon.

Figure 126 During the latter part of the bronze age more gods such as Poseidon took on human form and the animal forms were subsumed.

The gods of Mesopotamia and Egypt were often depicted as animals with part human form but with a clear relationship between god, man and animal. However in the Bronze Age this was set to change as Gods took on only human form and animals became subservient to them. So, as in the case of Poseidon, a human form is placed above an animal form linking the previous depiction of the God to the new version.

There are vases showing Poseidon on a horse which itself is sitting on a sea bull. This clearly shows the evolution of the god from his original bull form to that of the horse to one of human shape.

Figure 127 The Minoan snake goddess is an example of the mother goddess figure that held the highest status up until the rise of the new gods.

At a similar time, the Mother Goddess was being replaced by the Supreme male God. Eventually we have Athena springing out of the head of Zeus in full armour. The symbolism needs no explanation.

The cult of Zeus spread throughout the Aegean in the middle Bronze Age. Bull worship was no longer at the centre of the religion and the Gods had all taken on human form and behaviour. The slaying of the Minotaur is part of this. It seems this rise of the cult of Zeus paralleled the growth of Mycenaean power. In Crete and Cyprus, just as in Egypt, religion had animal stereotypes at its centre. The bull cult had reigned supreme in Crete in centres such as Knossos with the bull god. After the conquest by the Mycenaean's the Greek pantheon replaced the old religion. As with all religious changes the old forms were assimilated and adapted into the new religion to expedite and smooth its acceptance. Hence the new gods were shown astride the animal forms they replaced. Female and male gods had their own dominions.

The worship of Neith had long been established at Sais. She was a very ancient goddess and had been worshipped as far back as the 1st dynasty. She fulfilled various functions; one was as a goddess of war and another as a source of wisdom, when she was represented by an owl and also as goddess of the loom. She was also a Goddess of water (rivers ,lakes) and was mother of Isis (without the involvement of a partner, known as parthogenesis). These attributes of this deity led to her association with Athena, according to Herodotus and other sources close to the time when Solon visited Sais.

Figure 128 Excavation has recovered foundations of the city at Sais, but very little remains.

According to legend, Hor-Aha, a 1st Dynasty ruler founded a temple of Neith at Sais. By the time of Solon's (685-525bc) visit to Sais it had become the capital of Egypt in what this we call the Saite dynasty which flourished from 685 to 525bc and it seems probably that the temples at Sais would have rivalled those at Karnak for their size and opulence. This was an important link between Athens and Sais.

Archaeology has unearthed large amount of remains from around 1100bc and at some sites evidence of habitation stretching back to around 4000bc, by far the oldest found to date for the Nile delta. However, it does appear that around 1100bc that Sais became a much more significant centre and this would accord with the arrival of large numbers of foreigners seeking somewhere to settle and build new lives for themselves after the climatic disasters wrought on them in the north, the adoption of Neith as patron Goddess may have been related to this incursion

It seems that Sais increased in importance around 1100bc just as the 20th dynasty began to falter. In the reign of Ramses III (1185 to 1155bc estimated) during his 29th year (1156bc) there were labour strikes for the first time in Egyptian history when the elites could not be provisioned for which corresponds to the period of 2 decades in which something in the air arrested tree growth globally according to recent scientific studies.

As we have noted , Sais rose in importance to become the capitol of Egypt in the Saitic dynasty at the time Solon made his visit. However it was not to last and with the fall of this dynasty, Sais began a gradual decline until it was finally totally abandoned.

According to the Roman writer Proclus, who lived from 412 to 485 AD, the adyton (porch) of the temple at Sais bore the inscription which referred to the goddess Neith ' I am all that has been, all that is and all that ever will be, no mortal has yet lifted the veil from my face' . This is well known, however Proclus says in continues 'the fruit I bore is the Sun'.

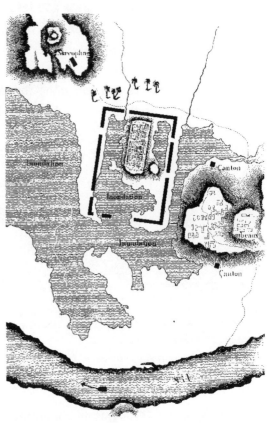

Figure 129 A map of the ancient city of Sais as drawn by the French archaeologist J.Champollion , one of the first explorers of the site

A senior official under King Cambyses who ruled Sais from 525 to 522bc , called Udjahorresne left records which tell of how we requested Cambyses to order the eviction of squatters who had built houses in the temple and for these houses to be destroyed and the temple to be returned to its former glory.   This tends to suggest that the records referred to by the priests would have been lost by this time, even though the temple was restored. The ruler after Cambyses was Darius who reigned from 521 to 486bc just before Herodotus was born. Herodotus records a large number of facts concerning the temple at Sais including a large obelisk, a sacred lake and the granite Naos of Amhose II. Much later, Lepsius in 19AD records that there were traces of a temple in an enclosure at Sais and that the temple had been destroyed in 14AD.   So it is evident that the inscriptions in Sias referred to in the dialogue had been lost long before Plato wrote his books.

Herodotus also noted that the citizens of Sais worshipped Neith and identified her with Athens and that she was the Egyptian goddess of wisdom. Another claim to fame for Sais was that the grave of Osiris the husband of Isis was on a nearby island in the delta. We now return to the subject of Greek mythology.

The stories of cyclops and giants who lived in the North appear in large number of myths. Famously Odysseus slew a cyclops, but they were a part of the world before the time of Zeus and according to legend had built the cyclopean walls around the Greek citadels. The origin of stories about one eyed men is

Figure130 Numerous gold and pottery objects found from this period, such as this Mycenaean cup, depict mythological scenes

most likely the same as the one eyed Arimispasians that Herodotus and others refer to, that is they were smiths who covered one eye in case of an accident when working metal. This practice has been common until recent times. The Greeks were people of small stature, probably little over 5ft tall. Skeletons from the Bronze Age of some north Europeans show they stood well over 6ft tall and were heavily built. It is easy to see how they appeared as giants to the Greeks of this time. Apollodorus describes them as 'long locks from head and chin, scales of dragons for feet and darting rocks and burning oaks at the sky'. In early Irish mythology, the Formorians get roughly the same treatment, with feet of scales of dragons, this simply being warm footwear suitable for the North as opposed to the Greeks, who generally wore sandals. In the Odyssey, the children of Poseidon were the giants and the also among the giants, the Cyclops. Giants were allies of Cronos in his war with Zeus, although some of the Cyclops may has assisted Zeus according to various accounts.

After the Trojan War and the collapse of Mycenae, myths record the Dorian invasion. These were supposedly Pelasgians (aboriginal peoples) who entered Attica from the North (Illyria). At around the same time another wandering group was the Heraclidae who moved from place to place before finally settling in various places. According to Livy, Antenor after the Trojan War joined the Erith and took land at the head of the Adriatic who became the Venetoi and according to Virgil, Padua was founded by Antenor, leader of the (V)Enetoi. All these mythical accounts confirm the large movements of populations around the end of the second millennium, which is borne out by the archaeological evidence.

In Northern Europe we have no myths that we can be sure date back to the Bronze Age. However the heroes of Asgard in their final battle rush out at Ragnarok to fight the wolf that consumes the sky but all perish and at a later time the artefacts of these gods are found buried in fields according to the legends. This

Figure 131 Caves such as the one at Delphi were seen as places of mystical or magical powers by bonze-age societies. Oracles would often occupy these places which would also include sacred groves and similar places.

does sound like a recollection of the events at the end of the Bronze Age. We also know that animals featured heavily in the myths of northern Europeans during the Bronze Age and many tales found in works such as the Irish mythological and cycle and the Mabinogion could recall some of these tails. The world tree Yggdrasil is another example of possibly a very ancient belief. Certainly, rivers, caves, wells, groves all played an important part in the beliefs of these peoples. The dominant gods were those of the sun, moon and the stars that they probably believed governed the seasons. Their rituals would have included large gatherings at which ritual processions, dances and ceremonies would have taken place accompanied by feasting and merrymaking. These aspects are common throughout almost all societies do would be expected. Morris dancing, horn dances, the maypole we see remnants of these festivals today.

Figure 132 Images from a bronze-age Scandinavian tomb. Many such rock carvings appear throughout Europe, Val Camonica in north Italy has thousands.

The symbols such as the wheel and spiral are possibly related to the sun and the chariots pulled by horses or birds feature either the sun disk or Poseidon (or Apollo) as a human image for the sun god. Like many ancient peoples they believed the sun was pulled across the sky every day and returned the following morning. Rituals would have been enacted to help fertility and for good harvests and the like. They may have believed the sky was held up by pillars and this would explain the presence of pillar cults in many locations. They clearly made offerings of animals such as bulls to placate the gods and would assume that deities held their fate in their hands.

Returning to the subject of myths, we all know the story of Arthur. How Uta Pendragon his father received the sword of power from the lady of the lake and as he died plunged it into a stone. How Arthur pulled Excalibur from the stone and then when he died in battle Merlin gave the sword back to the lady of the lake. Behind this story lie's some interesting truths. The lady of the lake was most likely the mother goddess who was also usually the goddess of water, particularly of rivers and lakes. There is much evidence that the symbols of power for kings were not a crown but a special sword. Hence we find many swords lying in river beds in the Bronze Age where they were given as offerings to the mother goddess or river goddess because of their special status. The giving and receiving of swords was of special significance.   We also have

evidence that important burials took place by a river when a chieftain or warrior was conveyed to their final burial place under a mound. The body of the dead king along with the priests and his successor would proceed by river to the burial ground where the dead king would be laid to rest in a mound such as that at Avebury. This is speculative, however, but is highly probable on the basis of the evidence

Figure 133 Stone ships such as this one at Badekunda are a common feature of this time and are thought assist the spirit of the dead in its journey to the otherworld.

we have.   Processions were a common event in antiquity at major festivals throughout the world and formed key parts of rituals as they defined social status as they do today. We know that Cursus's were in use from 3000bc, these defined the route taken by processions and form key elements of the traditions that enhanced the social cohesion of these disparate communities. Legends such as that of Arthur often contain a lot of lost detail about ancient rituals and give an idea of the value that mythology has in interpreting an ancient artefact.

The motions of the sun, moon, planets and stars were critical to their religious beliefs. Stonehenge was in part an astronomical instrument. The Aubrey stones could be used with only three stones to accurately predict eclipses. The stars were also seen as effecting events in the real world and so were studied intensely. The world pillar was a common feature to beliefs and supported the sky. The knowledge of the sky would have given power to the religious orders of the day and would have been combined with predictions based on many things. Location would have been important to impress believers, as with all religions, so places with atmosphere would have been selected, such as the cave at Delphi.

Berlin Golden hat Calendar: Measuring time in...

...solar months (30.4369 days)

									Zone 1
44	44	44	44	44	44	44	44	44	Zone 2
42	42	42	42	42	42	42	42	42	Zone 3
75	75	75	75	75	75	75	75	75	Zone 4
38	38	38		38	38	38		38	Zone 5
90	90	90	90	90	90	90	90	90	Zone 6
57	57	57	57	57		57		57	Zone 7
105	105	105	105	105	105	105	105	105	Zone 8
57	57	57	57	57	57	57	57	57	Zone 9
95	95	95	95	95	95	95	95	95	Zone 10
60	60	60	60	60	60	60	60	60	Zone 11
100	100	100	100	100	100	100	100	100	Zone 12
60	60	60	60	60	60	60	60	60	Zone 13
105	105	105	105	105	105	105	105	105	Zone 14
90	90	90	90	90	90	90	90	90	Zone 15
38	38	38	38	38	38	38	38	38	Zone 16
66	66	66		66		66	66	66	Zone 17
126	126	126	126	126	126	126	126	126	Zone 18
138	138	138	138	138	138	138	138	138	Zone 19
162	162	162	162	162	162	162	162	162	Zone 20
235	235	235	235	235	235	235	235	235	Zone 21
365	548	729	1100	1097	1461	1462	1644	1739	Sum
11.99	18.00	23.95	36.14	36.04	48.00	48.03	54.01	57.13	solar month
12	18	24	36	36	48	48	54	57	correct
0.07	0.02	0.20	0.39	0.12	0.00	0.07	0.02	0.24	error[%]

...synodic (lunar) months (29.5305 days)

Zone 1								
Zone 2	44	44	44	44	44	44	44	44
Zone 3	42	42	42	42	42	42	42	42
Zone 4	75	75	75	75	75	75	75	75
Zone 5	38		38		38		38	38
Zone 6	90	90	90	90	90	90	90	90
Zone 7		57		57	57	57	57	57
Zone 8	105	105	105	105	105	105	105	105
Zone 9	57	57	57	57	57	57	57	57
Zone 10	95	95	95	95	95	95	95	95
Zone 11	60	60	60	60	60	60	60	60
Zone 12	100	100	100	100	100	100	100	100
Zone 13	60	60	60	60	60	60	60	60
Zone 14	105	105	105	105	105	105	105	105
Zone 15	90	90	90	90	90	90	90	90
Zone 16	38	38	38	38	38	38	38	38
Zone 17	66			66	66		66	66
Zone 18	126	126	126	126	126	126	126	126
Zone 19	138	138	138	138	138	138	138	138
Zone 20	162	162	162	162	162	162	162	162
Zone 21	235	235	235	235	235	235	235	235
Sum	1682	1597	1423	1424	1059	1062	710	355
synod. month	56.96	54.08	48.19	48.22	35.86	35.96	24.04	12.02
correct	57	54	48	48	36	36	24	12
error[%]	0.07	0.15	0.39	0.46	0.39	0.10	0.18	0.18

Figure 134 The Conus hats found in south Germany featured very clever calendars that linked the solar and synodic calendars, as well as predicting the 19 year lunar cycle.

We know that satyrs in Greek myth are memories of the first time men on horseback appeared, a similar situation arose when Pizarro landed in South America in the 16th Century. The Inca had never seen a man on a horse and assumed it was one animal. When they dismounted it sent a shock wave through the Indians watching and they fled as they assumed one animal had broken into two living parts.

Unicorns are likewise the remembrance of Scythian horses that carried large brass horns fixed to their heads and so the list goes on. The Cyclops, who were one eyed giants, were actually smiths from central Europe. They would cover one eye in case of an accident when they were working and this ensured that they would still be able to see if something unforeseen during the course of their work happened. Stories like these probably came from travellers

We can invent imaginary animals such as dragons and griffins, so not all mythical creatures are real, however many are memories of real observations often misinterpreted. So as with the Greeks all we are left with are our myths.

Cecrops, Ericthonious and the other, early rulers of Athens mentioned in the dialogue were portrayed as anthropomorphic beings having the tail of a snake. Dragon's are an interesting case in point. The word for Dragon in Greek is Draco and in Anglo-Saxon and archaic German the word for a dragon is actually a snake or worm. The Snake in the sea myth and the snake that circles the world are among the oldest predating Summerian times. Angitia was an Umbrian Italian snake goddess of antiquity who was also the goddess of water and mentioned by Gnaeus Gellinus in 2nd century bc. The Prussians also worshipped a similar combined water snake god Potrimpo and snakes were revered anciently in Germany.

Figure 135 Snake worship in Egypt dates back far into antiquity

The worship of water and snakes is was extensive throughout the regions that formed the Atlantis confederation and indicates a common cult ancestry.

This worship of snakes also appears in Minoan figures such as the goddess idol unearthed at Knossos, as the Uraeus snake of the red crown of Lower Egypt and on the depictions of many Egyptian goddesses, such as Neith who wears this crown on her head. Bronze Age cauldrons carry snake images which show again that the snake was venerated in northern countries. The idea of a giant serpent in the sea dates to very ancient times both in Egypt and Europe. Since

142

antiquity the sea was believe--d to have characteristics associated with snakes. Kings of Athens later adopted Athena and then Zeus as their main gods and the cult of the snake and mother goddess was gradually replaced throughout much of the Mediterranean by dominant male Indo-European gods.

We are told that Cecrops came from Egypt and brought the worship of Neith with him. The highly approachable god Tithoes (Tutu) was the son of Neith in ancient Egypt and normally depicted with a human head, a lions body and the tail of a snake (like a sphinx). If Cecrops was the first to accept Zeus as a god it does not necessarily mean he accepted him as the supreme god. In fact Athena seems to have kept that position until the time of the war.

We have yet to decipher the symbols that appear on many megalithic structures and on rock faces across Europe. That they have significance is beyond doubt. The stone from Coilsfield, Ayrshire has been interpreted as showing three alternate rings of embankments and water around a holy place with access via a canal. This theme however occurs frequently so would have had a meaning. The whole looks

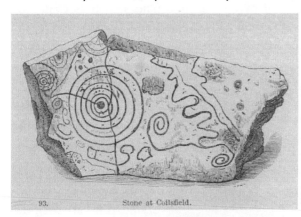

93.　　　Stone at Coilsfield.

Figure 136 A stone from Coilsfield shows a familiar arrangement of spirals, snake or river symbols and rings in a series.

like an attempt at a rough map with circles as villages, spirals and snake lines as rivers, but we can only guess. By the MBA the old megalithic religion had been replaced with a new pantheon of gods.

The names listed and the descriptions of the rituals given in the dialogue fit with the mythology. We have found blue cloaks and know bull worship was common throughout Europe and that more tyrannical societies appeared in the late Bronze Age just as Plato describes in his books.

Chapter 7

The Kingdoms of Atlantis

In the narratives recounted by Plato we are told that the main island was held by a king called Atlas, a title which passed down the generations. We are also told that the furthest part of the confederacy lay opposite Gadeira. The north of Africa by the Atlas Mountains was occupied by bell beaker traders during the bronze-age, so this would also fit with the facts as we know them. The other kingdoms could have included regions around places such as Gadeira, Brittany, The Netherlands around the Rhine delta and Germany/Denmark by the Elba, southern Britain, Scandinavia, Salzburg region and Sardinia and/or Sicily.

Figure 137 The Adige valley winds its way through the alps creating a natural corridor for trade from northern Europe into the Adriatic and onto the kingdoms around the shores of the Mediterranean Sea.

There is considerable evidence that all these places were connected together by trade in a loose confederation of states. The absence of large settlements does not present a problem to this hypothesis as power in such societies was very diffuse. Unlike the middle-east, in Europe vertical power structures were rare in ancient times and kings only held power tenuously. They were often elected and could be removed and replaced if they failed to perform. Even in Britain up until Tudor times, Barons had their own armies and decided whether or not they would join in common enterprises on the basis of what they might get out of it. In theory the Kings rule was absolute in practice it was a hollow crown.

Practically, much of Northern Europe was heavily wooded and if someone wished to hide it was easy to do so, unlike Egypt were you were always easy to spot. Thus required a different approach to how society operated which still partly applies to this day.

Ceremonies, religious and otherwise, brought people together. However there were no such things as fairs at this time. So barter would have been the way goods exchanged hands, the traders would always be at risk of ambush and the villagers of pillaging. However, wealth did congregate in the hands of the powerful rich landowners and traders who would have had their own armies to protect them and advance their interests. It is the elite that concerned itself with conquest and empire building, each little fiefdom could join in a common campaign if the incentive was sufficient. We therefore are not looking at the same types of armies that the Hittites and Egyptians had, but that did not make them less effective. In many ways, it gave an advantage to the northerners, as they would have been involved in the main because they wanted to be. The Vikings conquered much of Europe with such a loose confederation.

Figure 138 Large settlements such as this in Sardinia in the bronze-age were a feature of these regions

The whole of the Po plain was turned over to agriculture and according to the narrative, this kingdom did have an organised army. In northern Italy the Terramare culture was preceded by what we call the Polada culture, 1800-1600bc. In Sardinia a culture called the Bonnanaro culture flourished from around 1800 to 1600bc. It had a lot of similarities to the Polada culture and is seen as the first stage of what is known as the Nuraghe civilisation.

Figure 139 A settlement from the bronze-age in Sicily typical of many on the island

The Nuragic built large stone towers throughout Sardinia, Today over 7000 of them still remain. Who built these towers was a mystery to the Greeks who attributed them to Daedalus. During the next centuries Sardinia became a huge centre of metal production in the Mediterranean. Tin was sourced from Cornwall and Iberia and Sardinia itself was a large source of Copper and other metals. Among its markets were Mycaenae, Cyprus, Crete and Iberia . It was probably the most advanced civilisation in the western Mediterranean at this time. The use of the towers is disputed, they could have been defensive or alternatively for storage or even possibly religious. The only structures similar to them are in Corsica. However, there are also remains clearly connected with water gods. Statues of the warriors show them wearing horned helmets and in the records of the Sea Peoples, the Sherden (or Shardana) have been identified

Figure 140 The bronze-age Monkodoja site near to Rovigo in Istria has evidence of an acropolis and palace within the walled enclosure

with them and they wear this same dress. Their chiefs are depicted wearing a cloak, hat and weapon in line with chiefs of this period. The presence of so many forts also tells us that the population was high for these times and that they would have been very wealthy for the time. The development of the Nuraghe culture around 1600bc also tells us that trade must have stepped up a notch in the Mediterranean. This time also coincides with the rise of the tumulus culture and the warrior society.

The pre Sardis name for Sardinia, was according to legend Stepping Stone in local language. This would have applied to Majorca and to the east Sicily. Majorca has many megalithic sites such as found in Sardinia and Taula's, which are large pillars with capstones that often sit within a circle.

Figure 141 Across Majorca there are many bronze-age sites , some feature a column called a Taula such as seen in this image. Possibly a world pillar symbol.

Sicily similarly has many bronze-age sites as does Istria with its Castellera. Brittany has Mont Michel and Cornwall, St Michaels mount, which would both have been defensive positions.

We also have evidence of cities in the Hungarian plain which are surrounded by defensive stone walls. However, many European villages were built in lakes or with rings of water around them and presumably wooden stockades, which served the same purpose. Hill forts were also very common until the LBA.

The mounds of the bog people in Denmark show a wealthy pastoral society as does the post Wessex, Urnfield villages in Britain which contained up to 60 round houses within a stockade surrounded by fields laid out in regular patterns.

We know a reasonable amount about the Nugaric society in Sardinia. Research has shown that it was marked by well-defined social classes. Bronzes show chiefs with their cloaks and hats, they also depict miners and artisans and the large military class, with archers, infantry men swordsmen, musicians and boxers depicted. Women wore their hair long and men generally had short hair sometimes covered by a thin cap. Their religion contained both male and female deities. The bull had been worshipped from antiquity and the male bull-son god appears alongside the female moon-water goddess. They had special holy places where they gathered characterised by temples with a pit inside and steps around it. A similar sacred pit temple was found in western Bulgaris near the town of Garlo. There are also many megalithic tombs of this period, the have large stones and a group outside the tomb forming a gathering area. Similar such tombs appear throughout megalithic northern Europe and close to Aberdeen there similar tombs with porticoes. A recent study of 71 Swedish bronze objects of this time revealed that the copper used in them had come from Sardinia or Iberia. The connection between the Nuragic culture and other tumulus cultures is clear and gives us an insight into the general culture of the larger trading empire. The buildings the Nugaric made are certainly the equal of those of the Mycaenae and of the Minoans of this time. There is however, no indication that writing was

Figure 142 Early bronze-age sites such as Los Millares in southern Spain show a continuity of architecture within the bell beaker and evolved cultures.

used by the Nugaric and it seems that there are therefore no written records of these peoples to be uncovered.

The Unetice culture of central Europe flourished from around 2300 to around 1600bc. It was characterised by very large burial mounds showing great wealth. It had two phases from2300 to 1950bc and from 1950bc to 1600bc. It controlled Balkan and Alpine copper deposits and Bohemian tin resources, it also controlled the Amber trade routes. Links could be shown with places as far apart as Alsace and Ugarit with examples such as massive Torcs. These had ends that are hammered and curled round and so are quite distinctive. The Unetice were heavily influenced if not evolved from the Bell Beaker culture.

There temples were made of wood and not stone and they seem to have developed the oak coffins that are familiar in the Danish bronze-age burials,

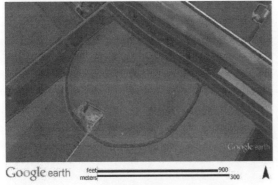

typified by the Egtved woman. There are copies of wares produced by both the Unetice and the Mycaenaens , but it is not clear as to whom copies whom. The Polada culture shows signs of newly arrived eastern immigrants in around 2nd milleinium bc who brought

Figure 143 Bronze age fort at Veronella Alta dated 1800 to 1200bc near the ancient course of the Adige River similar to Castelleria at Monkodonja, Istria

metalworking with them. The Unetice culture gave way to the Tumulus culture, which in turn evolved into the Urnfield culture. These changes do not seem to have been invasions but rather a change in society wrought from within.

There are remnants of a large Bronze Age fort or Castelleri at Veronella , which is south-east of Verona. It is located very close to the ancient course of the Adige River and would have neen a short distance upriver from the towns of Montagna, Este and Monselice. The embankment of the fort measures over 1500x900 feet and is roughly elliptical in shape. It is very similar in appearance to the casterlleri at Monkodonja in Istria. The site at Veronalla is aligned to the winter solctice and appears to have had some religious of cult significance. It can be clearly seen as it is defined by a very substantial earth rampart. The fort wad in use from 1800 to 1200bc and would have been active during the period of the Atlanteans.

It has been clearly shown that there were strong connections between the northern Adriatic and the Mycenae at the time of the events Plato describes. Thre is clear evidence that the site in Monkodonja was trading with Mycenae. There is also clear evidence that the Este was also trading with these placesin the late Bronze Age and there are clear similarities between the po[ulation iof Istria and the so called Este or Atlantean peoples at this time.

The Casterlleri of Monkodonja is enclosed by a stone wall and has a palace within in which there are many post holes showing large numbers of pillars were used. Outside the wall there is a cave which was probably a sacred well. The site in general clearly fit the description of the temple in the dialogue.

There are a large number of castelleri dating from the Bronze Age in Istria which are close together , so it would be likely that the fort at Veronella was not unique and that other forts would have been placed along the Adige towards the sea.

Sometime during the late Bronze Age as more organised societies arose a number of confederations must have formed with the

Figure 144 The complexity of the houses at Skara Brae shows that thousands of years before the events we are looking into and before any buildings were constructed in Egypt , that in the north buildings such as this and many others were being constructed

aim of protecting mutual trade interests. The Atlantean confederation was one of these. The war between Zeus and Chronos was a memory of the conflict between the Atlantean and formative Greek world that evolved into what we call the Mycenaen empire and these conflicts continued up to the Trojan War.

All the evidence: archaeological, historical and mythological points to the existence of well organised societies across much of Europe and among larger Mediterranean islands in the later Bronze Age. This had arisen as trade had taken over as the key source of wealth from agriculture and was mirrored in the rise of warrior type societies with more hierarchical structures. The building of major forts required the effective management of large numbers of people and indicates larger population densities within Europe with greater interaction than have formerly been assumed. The forming of alliances among these separate societies would have served to protect their interests and would have been necessary to facilitate stable trade routes over long distances. The trade between Europe and the Mediterranean peaked during the late Bronze Age and at a later date severe climate events coupled with internal conflicts led to the collapse of trade throughout Europe and the Mediterranean and a dark age which continued into the first millennium.

Chapter 8

Plato's legacy

One of the greatest problems with the North European Bronze Age is that we do not have an Herodotus, Livy, Pliny, Strabo or Diodorus Sicula let alone a Pausanias to tell us about the people and the events of the period. We are forced to construct a very approximate history from the range of archaeological discoveries that we have found along with a small number of inscriptions and a lot of later mythology which has been wrapped up in religious doctrine or distorted for a wide range of reasons including political and ideological ones.

So, the existence of a work that gives a detailed account of a major European society in the latter part of the Bronze Age has considerable value if it can be shown to have substance and be predominantly correct.

From my analysis, I believe the account rendered by Plato was in the main a pretty accurate account of events and the societies involved in Europe around 1350bc. I also believe that much of the Ancient Greek literature that still survives and dates from a time much closer to the one we are considering contains a great deal of factual material.

At the present, such sources are all we have to go on. However, many recent checks have repeatedly shown the surprising accuracy of information within these written sources. Herodotus, once called the king of all liars, to a large extent has been vindicated. Richard Schliemann took the Iliad at face value and discovered Troy. Arthur Evans likewise accepted the stories of Minos and revealed Knossos to the world. Pausanias, the Roman Baedeker Guide, is packed full of incredibly valuable content much of which has yet to be explored properly. Plato, one of the greatest philosophers, also told the truth in his dialog. We should not be surprised if this is the case, as in their culture, remembering large amounts of detail was an art they would have practised for decades and would have been probably more accomplished than anyone today as they did not have the technology to access which removed the needs for these skills. In our own time, it may be that simple mathematical skills disappear as technology makes our need to use them redundant.

This dark-age lasted for anything from a hundred to several hundred years. Some regions, such as Britain were less effected but overall trade ceased and just as the monks at Sais had explained, memories of the old ways and their institutions and history had all but vanished , preserved only as verbally recited myth, as they served no purpose in this new world order. Education is a luxury of well organised societies. These new societies placed much greater emphasis on the use of brute force in warfare to achieve their goals.

Needless to say they were not very successful and it would not be until the arrival of new groups such as the Druids and Bards who valued knowledge, that a return to organised societies would occur. In Italy the Etruscans emerged by around 800bc and in Greece from about the same time, the seeds of the Hellenistic period were being sown. In Europe the Hallstatt culture appears and the Phoenicians build a new trading empire throughout the Mediterranean. In the Middle East, new kingdoms appear to replace those of the Hittites and the Assyrian Empire reaches the height of its power before falling to the Achaemedians under Cyrus.

The most likely scenario is that a long period of drought followed the end of the Trojan War and this was coupled with a series of earthquakes. Then at a later time, maybe 1160bc an extremely wet and colder period began which particularly hit north Europe and possibly was a result of Hekla. At some stage during this time a meteor or comet passed very close to earth and sent large number s of asteroids falling to earth. This was remembered as Phaeton and in the fall of Aasgard and many other places. However, it is very unlikely that the comet actually caused the climate change but it is possible it could have triggered the earthquakes but it may just have been an un-connected or co-incidental event but assumed to be the cause as the events.

All religions have assimilated old beliefs to facilitate their acceptance and in some cases to shown the subsuming of the old order by the new. Churches were built in early times within stone circles, harvest festival replaced Beltaine, (which was really an ancestor worship ceremony which has now become Halloween). The true history of the victory achieved by Zeus became modified to fit a religious doctrine. We are told Cecrops was the first to name Zeus a

God and no doubt a cult rapidly built up around him. It is also a time when female goddesses are being either replaced or subsumed beneath male gods, and so while Athena remains a female warrior God her status is lowered and Zeus became the top God.

With the rise of the cult of Zeus, the legends were adapted and true history behind the war and that of the kingdom of Atlantis disappeared almost completely, so when Solon made his visit to Egypt, the story he was told was a complete revelation to him.

Plato lived at a remarkable time in human history. Two centuries earlier Zoroastianism had swept throughout the Middle East with the rise of the Achaemenid Empire when Cyrus had overthrown Belshazzar in 539bc. This also allowed Jews in Babylon such as Ezra the intellectual freedom to complete the writing of the Bible. Buddha's teaching had spread throughout the Far East, and Pythagoras had founded the cult of the Pythagoreans, philosophy when this subject was in its infancy as well as starting a mathematical renaissance. The first democratic government had arisen in Athens, even though it was not a formod democracy we might recognise, it is a mark of how far Greece had progressed. This climate produced new ideas and allowed the questioning of older ones but only up to a point.

It is in this climate that intellectuals such as Plato, Aristotle, Socrates were able to develop their ideas. Among Plato's greatest concerns was the nature of society and how it could be improved. The works Timaeus and Critias are very important landmarks in the development of human thought.

While we may not agree with everything Plato has said and that science has overtaken his interpretation of natural phenomena, I believe that when he says that this particular story is in his opinion a true account he was not telling a lie.

He clearly believed that the story passed down by Solon was historically accurate and I believe I have proved that this is true.

Appendix – Plato's narrative

Plato's narrative is in two parts, the first comes from his work Timaeus and the second is from his incomplete work Critias. This version is from the original one used by Ignatius Donelly. However almost all the translations are very close and the most popular one is the Penguin version translated by Desmond Lee.

The Timaeus dialogue

Critias. Then listen, Socrates, to a strange tale, which is, however, certainly true, as Solon, who was the wisest of the seven sages, declared. He was a relative and great friend of my great-grandfather, Dropidas, as be himself says in several of his poems; and Dropidas told Critias, my grandfather, who remembered, and told us, that there were of old great and marvellous actions of the Athenians, which have passed into oblivion through time and the destruction of the human race and one in particular, which was the greatest of them all, the recital of which will be a suitable testimony of our gratitude to you....

Socrates. Very good; and what is. this ancient famous action of which Critias spoke, not as a mere legend, but as a veritable action of the Athenian State, which Solon recounted!

Critias. I will tell an old-world story which I heard from an aged man; for Critias was, as be said, at that time nearly ninety years of age, and I was about ten years of age. Now the day was that day of the Apaturia which is called the registration of youth; at which, according to custom, our parents gave prizes for recitations, and the poems of several poets were recited by us boys, and many of us sung the poems of Solon, which were new at the time. One of our tribe, either because this was his real opinion, or because he thought that he would please Critias, said that, in his judgment, Solon was not only the wisest of men but the noblest of poets. The old man, I well remember, brightened up at this, and said, smiling: "Yes, Amynander, if Solon had only, like other poets, made poetry the business of his life, and had completed the tale which he brought with him from Egypt, and had not been compelled, by reason of the factions and troubles which he found stirring in this country when he came home, to attend to other matters, in my opinion be would have been as famous as Homer, or Hesiod, or any poet."

"And what was that poem about, Critias?" said the person who addressed him.

"About the greatest action which the Athenians ever did, and which ought to have been the most famous, but which, through the lapse of time and the death of those who took part, has not come down to us."

"Tell us," said the other, "the whole story, and how and from whom Solon heard this veritable tradition."

He replied: "At the head of the Egyptian Delta, where the river Nile divides, there is a certain district which is called the district of Sais, and the great city of the district is also called Sais, and is the city from which Amasis the king was sprung. And the citizens have a deity who is their foundress: she is called in the Egyptian tongue Neith, which is asserted by them to be the same whom the Hellenes called Athene. Now, the citizens of this city are great lovers of the Athenians, and say that they are in some way related to them. Thither came Solon, who was received by them with great honor; and be asked the priests, who were most skilful in such matters, about antiquity, and made the discovery that neither he nor any other Hellene knew anything worth mentioning about the times of old. On one occasion, when he was drawing them on to speak of antiquity, he began to tell about the most ancient things in our part of the world--about Phoroneus, who is called 'the first,' and about Niobe; and, after the Deluge, to tell of the lives of Deucalion and Pyrrha; and he traced the genealogy of their descendants, and attempted to reckon bow many years old were the events of which he was speaking, and to give the dates. Thereupon, one of the priests, who was of very great age; said, 'O Solon, Solon, you Hellenes are but children, and there is never an old man who is an Hellene.' Solon, bearing this, said, 'What do you mean?' 'I mean to say,' he replied, 'that in mind you are all young; there is no old opinion handed down among you by ancient tradition, nor any science which is hoary with age. And I will tell you the reason of this: there have been, and there will be again, many destructions of mankind arising out of many causes. There is a story which even you have preserved, that once upon a time Phaëthon, the son of Helios, having yoked the steeds in

155

his father's chariot, because he was not able to drive them in the path of his father, burnt up all that was upon the earth, and was himself destroyed by a thunderbolt. Now, this has the form of a myth, but really signifies a declination of the bodies moving around the earth and in the heavens, and a great conflagration of things upon the earth recurring at long intervals of time: when this happens, those who live upon the mountains and in dry and lofty places are more liable to destruction than those who dwell by rivers or on the sea-shore; and from this calamity the Nile, who is our never-failing saviour, saves and delivers us. When, on the other hand, the gods purge the earth with a deluge of water, among you herdsmen and shepherds on the mountains are the survivors, whereas those of you who live in cities are carried by the rivers into the sea; but in this country neither at that time nor at any other does the water come from above on the fields, having always a tendency to come up from below, for which reason the things preserved here are said to be the oldest. The fact is, that wherever the extremity of winter frost or of summer sun does not prevent, the human race is always increasing at times, and at other times diminishing in numbers. And whatever happened either in your country or in ours, or in any other region of which we are informed--if any action which is noble or great, or in any other way remarkable has taken place, all that has been written down of old, and is preserved in our temples; whereas you and other nations are just being provided with letters and the other things which States require; and then, at the usual period, the stream from heaven descends like a pestilence, and leaves only those of you who are destitute of letters and education; and thus you have to begin all over again as children, and know nothing of what happened in ancient times, either among us or among yourselves. As for those genealogies of yours which you have recounted to us, Solon, they are no better than the tales of children; for, in the first place, you remember one deluge only, whereas there were many of them; and, in the next place, you do not know that there dwelt in your land the fairest and noblest race of men which ever lived, of whom you and your whole city are but a seed or remnant. And this was unknown to you, because for many generations the survivors of that destruction died and made no sign. For there was a time, Solon, before that great deluge of all, when the city which now is Athens was first in war, and was preeminent for the excellence of her laws, and is said to have performed the noblest deeds, and to have had the fairest constitution of any of which tradition tells, under the face of heaven.' Solon marvelled at this, and earnestly requested the priest to inform him exactly and in order about these former citizens. 'You are welcome to hear about them, Solon,' said the priest, 'both for your own sake and for that of the city; and, above all, for the sake of the goddess who is the common patron and protector and educator of both our cities. She founded your city a thousand years before ours, receiving from the Earth and Hephæstus the seed of your race, and then she founded ours, the constitution of which is set down in our sacred registers as 8000 years old. As touching the citizens of 9000 years ago, I will briefly inform you of their laws and of the noblest of their actions; and the exact particulars of the whole we will hereafter go through at our leisure in the sacred registers themselves. If you compare these very laws with your own, you will find that many of ours are the counterpart of yours, as they were in the olden time. In the first place, there is the caste of priests, which is separated from all the others; next there are the artificers, who exercise their several crafts by themselves, and without admixture of any other; and also there is the class of shepherds and that of hunters, as well as that of husbandmen; and you will observe, too, that the warriors in Egypt are separated from all the other classes, and are commanded by the law only to engage in war; moreover, the weapons with which they are equipped are shields and spears, and this the goddess taught first among you, and then in Asiatic countries, and we among the Asiatics first adopted.

"'Then, as to wisdom, do you observe what care the law took from the very first, searching out and comprehending the whole order of things down to prophecy and medicine (the latter with a view to health); and out of these divine elements drawing what was needful for human life, and adding every sort of knowledge which was connected with them. All this order and arrangement the goddess first imparted to you when establishing your city; and she chose the spot of earth in which you were born, because she saw that the happy temperament of the seasons in that land would produce the wisest of men. Wherefore the goddess, who was a lover both of war and of wisdom, selected, and first of all settled that spot which was the most likely to produce men likest herself. And there you dwelt, having such laws as these and still better ones, and excelled all mankind in all virtue, as became the children and disciples of the gods. Many great and wonderful deeds are recorded of your State in our histories; but one of them exceeds all the rest in greatness and valour; for these histories tell of a mighty power which was aggressing wantonly against the whole of Europe and Asia, and to which your city put an end. This power came forth out of the Atlantic Ocean, for in those days the Atlantic was navigable; and there was an island situated in front of the straits which you call the Columns of Heracles: the island was larger than Libya and Asia put together, and was the way to other islands, and from the islands you might pass through the whole of the opposite continent which surrounded the true ocean; for this sea which is within the Straits of Heracles is only a harbour, having a narrow entrance, but that other is a real sea, and the surrounding land may be most truly called a continent. Now, in the island of Atlantis there was a great and wonderful empire, which had rule over the whole island and several others, as well as over parts of the continent; and, besides these, they subjected the parts of Libya within the Columns of Heracles as far as Egypt, and of Europe as far as Tyrrhenia. The vast power thus gathered into one, endeavoured to subdue at one blow our country and yours, and the whole of the land which was within the straits; and then, Solon, your country shone forth, in the excellence of her virtue and strength, among all mankind; for she was the first in courage and military skill, and was the leader of the Hellenes. And when the rest fell off from her, being compelled to stand alone, after having undergone the very extremity of danger, she defeated and triumphed over the invaders, and preserved from slavery those who were not yet subjected, and freely liberated all the others who dwelt within the limits of Heracles. But afterward there occurred violent earthquakes and floods, and in a single day and night of rain all your warlike men in a body sunk into the earth, and the island of Atlantis in like manner disappeared, and was sunk beneath the sea. And that is the reason why the sea in those parts is impassable and impenetrable, because there is such a quantity of shallow mud in the way; and this was caused by the subsidence of the island.' ("Plato's Dialogues," ii., 617, *Timæus*.) . . .

The Critias dialogue

"But in addition to the gods whom you have mentioned, I would specially invoke Mnemosyne; for all the important part of what I have to tell is dependent on her favour, and if I can recollect and recite enough of what was said by the priests, and brought hither by Solon, I doubt not that I shall satisfy the requirements of this theatre. To that task, then, I will at once address myself.

"Let me begin by observing, first of all, that nine thousand was the sum of years which had elapsed since the war which was said to have taken place between all those who dwelt outside the Pillars of Heracles and those who dwelt within them: this war I am now to describe. Of the combatants on the one side the city of Athens was reported to have been the ruler, and to have directed the contest; the combatants on the other side were led by the kings of the islands of Atlantis, which, as I was saying, once had an extent greater than that of Libya and Asia; and, when afterward sunk by an earthquake, became an impassable barrier of mud to voyagers sailing from hence to the ocean. The progress of the history will unfold the various tribes of barbarians and Hellenes which then existed, as they successively appear on the scene; but I must begin by describing, first of all, the Athenians as they were in that day, and their enemies who fought with them; and I shall have to tell of the power and form of government of both of them. Let us give the precedence to Athens. . . .

Many great deluges have taken place during the nine thousand years, for that is the number of years which have elapsed since the time of which I am speaking; and in all the ages and changes of things there has never been any settlement of the earth flowing down from the mountains, as in other places, which is worth speaking of; it has always been carried round in a circle, and disappeared in the depths below. The consequence is that, in comparison of what then was, there are remaining in small islets only the bones of the wasted body, as they may be called, all the richer and softer parts of the soil having fallen away, and the mere skeleton of the country being left. . . .

"And next, if I have not forgotten what I heard when I was a child, I will impart to you the character and origin of their adversaries; for friends should not keep their stories to themselves, but have them in common. Yet, before proceeding farther in the narrative, I ought to warn you that you must not be surprised if you should bear Hellenic names given to foreigners. I will tell you the reason of this: Solon, who was intending to use the tale for his poem, made an investigation into the meaning of the names, and found that the early Egyptians, in writing them down, had translated them into their own language, and he recovered the meaning of the several names and retranslated them, and copied them out again in our language. My great-grandfather, Dropidas, had the original writing, which is still in my possession, and was carefully studied by me when I was a child. Therefore, if you bear names such as are used in this country, you must not be surprised, for I have told you the reason of them.

"The tale, which was of great length, began as follows: I have before remarked, in speaking of the allotments of the gods, that they distributed the whole earth into portions differing in extent, and made themselves temples and sacrifices. And Poseidon, receiving for his lot the island of Atlantis, begat children by a mortal woman, and settled them in a part of the island which I will proceed to describe. On the side toward the sea, and in the centre of the whole island, there was a plain which is said to have been the fairest of all plains, and very fertile. Near the plain again, and also in the centre of the island, at a distance of about fifty stadia, there was a hill of no great size. In this hill there dwelt one of the earth-born primeval men of that country, whose name was Evenor, and he had a wife named Leucippe, and they had an only daughter, who was named Cleito. The maiden was growing up to womanhood when her father and mother died; Poseidon fell in love with her, and had intercourse with her; and, breaking the ground, enclosed the hill in which she dwelt all round, making alternate zones of sea and land, larger and smaller, encircling one another; there were two of land and three of water, which he turned as with a lathe out of the centre of the island, equidistant every way, so that no man could get to the island, for ships and voyages were not yet heard of. He himself, as be was a god, found no difficulty in making special arrangements for the centre island, bringing two streams of water under the earth, which he caused to ascend as springs, one of warm water and the other of cold, and making every variety of food to spring up abundantly in the earth. He also begat and brought up five pairs of male children, dividing the island of Atlantis into ten portions: he gave to the first-born of the eldest pair his mother's dwelling and the surrounding allotment, which was the largest and best, and made him king over the rest; the others he made princes, and gave them rule over many men and a large territory. And he named them all: the eldest, who was king, he named Atlas, and from him the whole island and the ocean received the name of Atlantic. To his twin-brother, who was born after him, and obtained as his lot the extremity of the island toward the Pillars of Heracles, as far as the country which is still called the region of Gades in that part of the world, be gave the name which in the Hellenic language is Eumelus, in the language of the country which is named after him, Gadeirus. Of the second pair of twins, he called one Ampheres and the other Evæmon. To the third pair of twins he gave the name Mneseus to the elder, and Autochthon to the one who followed him. Of the fourth pair of twins he called the elder Elasippus and the younger Mestor, And of the fifth pair be gave to the elder the name of Azaes, and to the younger Diaprepes. All these and their descendants were the inhabitants and rulers of diverse islands in the open sea; and also, as has been already said, they held sway in the other direction over the country within the Pillars as far as Egypt and Tyrrhenia. Now Atlas had a numerous and honourable family, and his eldest branch always retained the kingdom, which the eldest son handed on to his eldest for many generations; and they had such an amount of wealth as was never before possessed by kings and potentates, and is not likely ever to be again, and they were furnished with everything which they could have, both in city and country. For, because of the greatness of their empire, many things were brought to them from foreign countries, and the island itself provided much of what was required by them for the uses of life. In the first place, they dug out of the earth whatever was to be found there, mineral as well as metal, and that which is now only a name, and was then something more than a name--orichalcum--was dug out of the earth in many parts of the island, and, with the exception of gold, was esteemed the most precious of metals among the men of those days. There was an abundance of wood for carpenters' work, and sufficient maintenance for tame and wild animals. Moreover, there were a great number of elephants in the island, and there was provision for animals of every kind, both for those which live in lakes and marshes and rivers, and also for those which live in mountains and on plains, and therefore for the animal which is the largest and most voracious of them. Also, whatever fragrant things there are in the earth, whether roots, or herbage, or woods, or distilling drops of flowers or fruits, grew and thrived in that land; and again, the cultivated fruit of the earth, both the dry edible fruit and other species of food, which we call by the general name of legumes, and the fruits having a hard rind, affording drinks, and meats, and ointments, and good store of chestnuts and the like, which may be used to play with, and are fruits which spoil with keeping--and the pleasant kinds of dessert which console us after dinner, when we are full and tired of eating--all these that sacred island lying beneath the sun brought forth fair and wondrous in infinite abundance. All these things they received from the earth, and they employed themselves in constructing their temples, and palaces, and harbours, and docks; and they arranged the whole country in the following manner: First of all they bridged over the zones of sea which surrounded the ancient metropolis, and made a passage into and out of it they began to build a palace in the place where the god and their ancestors had lived. This they continued to ornament in successive generations, every king surpassing the one who came before him to the utmost of his power, until they made the building a marvel to behold for size and for beauty. And, beginning from the sea, they dug a canal three hundred feet in width and one hundred feet in depth, and fifty stadia in length, which they carried through to the outermost zone, making a passage from the sea up to this, which became a harbour, and leaving an opening sufficient to enable the largest vessels to find ingress. Moreover, they divided the zones of land which parted the zones of sea, constructing bridges of such a width as would leave a passage for a single trireme to pass out of one into another, and roofed them over; and there was a way underneath for the ships, for the banks of the zones were raised considerably above the water. Now the largest of the zones into which a passage was cut from the sea was three stades in breadth, and the zone of land which came next of equal breadth; but the next two, as well the zone of water as of land, were two stades, and the one which surrounded the central island was a stadium only in width. The island in which the palace was situated had a diameter of five stades. This, and the zones and the bridge, which was the sixth part of a stadium in width, they surrounded by a stone wall, on either side placing towers, and gates on the bridges where the sea passed in. The stone which was used in the work they quarried from underneath the centre island and from underneath the zones, on the outer as well as the inner side. One kind of stone was white, another black, and a third red; and, as they quarried, they at the same time hollowed out docks double within, having roofs formed out of the native rock. Some of their buildings were simple, but in others they put together different stones, which they intermingled for the sake of ornament, to be a natural source of delight. The entire circuit of the wall which went round the outermost one they covered with a coating of bronze, and the circuit of the next wall they coated with tin, and the third, which encompassed the citadel flashed with the red light of orichalcum. The palaces in the interior of the citadel were constructed in this wise: In the centre was a holy temple dedicated to Cleito and Poseidon, which remained inaccessible, and was surrounded by an enclosure of gold; this was the spot in which they originally begat the race of the ten princes, and thither they annually brought the fruits of the earth in their season from all the ten portions, and performed sacrifices to each of them. Here, too, was Poiseidon's own temple, of a stadium in length and half a stadium in width, and of a proportionate height, having a sort of barbaric splendour. All the outside of the temple, with the exception of the pinnacles, they covered with silver, and the pillars with gold. In the interior of the temple the roof was of ivory, adorned everywhere with gold and silver and orichalcum; all the other parts of the walls and pillars and floor they lined with orichalcum. In the temple they placed statues of gold: there was the god himself standing in a chariot--the charioteer of six winged horses--and of such a size that he touched the roof of the building with his head; around him there were a hundred Nereids riding on dolphins, for such was thought to be the number of them in that day. There were also in the interior of the temple other images which had been dedicated by private individuals. And around the temple on the outside were placed statues of gold of all the ten kings and of their wives; and there were many other great offerings, both of kings and of private individuals, coming both from the city itself and the foreign cities over which they held sway. There was an altar, too, which in size and workmanship corresponded to the rest of the work, and there were palaces in like manner which answered to the greatness of the kingdom and the glory of the temple.

"In the next place, they used fountains both of cold and hot springs; these were very abundant, and both kinds wonderfully adapted to use by reason of the sweetness and excellence of their waters. They constructed buildings about them, and planted suitable trees; also cisterns, some open to the heaven, other which they roofed over, to be used in winter as warm baths, there were the king's baths, and the baths of private persons, which were kept apart; also separate baths for women, and others again for horses and cattle, and to them they gave as much adornment as was suitable for them. The water which ran off they carried, some to the grove of Poseidon, where were growing all manner of trees of wonderful height and beauty, owing to the excellence of the soil; the remainder was conveyed by aqueducts which passed over the bridges to the outer circles: and there were many temples built and dedicated to many gods; also gardens and places of exercise, some for men, and some set apart for horses, in both of the two islands formed by the zones; and in the centre of the larger of the two there was a race-course of a stadium in width, and in length allowed to extend all-round the island, for horses to race in. Also there were guard-houses at intervals for the body-guard, the more trusted of whom had their duties appointed to them in the lesser zone, which was nearer the Acropolis; while the most trusted of all had houses given them within the citadel, and about the persons of the kings. The docks were full of triremes and naval stores, and all things were quite ready for use. Enough of the plan of the royal palace. Crossing the outer harbours, which were three in number, you would come to a wall which began at the sea and went all round: this was everywhere distant fifty stadia from the largest zone and harbour, and enclosed the whole, meeting at the mouth of the channel toward the sea. The entire area was densely crowded with habitations; and the canal and the largest of the harbours were full of vessels and merchants coming from all parts, who, from their numbers, kept up a multitudinous sound of human voices and din of all sorts night and day. I have repeated his descriptions of the city and the parts about the ancient palace nearly as he gave them, and now I must endeavour to describe the nature and arrangement of the rest of the country. The whole country was described as being very lofty and precipitous on the side of the sea, but the country immediately about and surrounding the city was a level plain, itself surrounded by mountains which descended toward the sea; it was smooth and even, but of an oblong shape, extending in one direction three thousand stadia, and going up the country from the sea through the centre of the island two thousand stadia; the whole region of the island lies toward the south, and is sheltered from the north. The surrounding mountains he celebrated for their number and size and beauty, in which they exceeded all that are now to be seen anywhere; having in them also many wealthy inhabited villages, and rivers and lakes, and meadows supplying food enough for every animal, wild or tame, and wood of various sorts, abundant for every kind of work. I will now describe the plain, which had been cultivated during many ages by many generations of kings. It was rectangular, and for the most part straight and oblong; and what it wanted of the straight line followed the line of the circular ditch. The depth and width and length of this ditch were incredible and gave the impression that such a work, in addition to so many other works, could hardly have been wrought by the hand of man. But I must say what I have heard. It was excavated to the depth of a hundred feet, and its breadth was a stadium everywhere; it was carried round the whole of the plain, and was ten thousand stadia in length. It received the streams which came down from the mountains, and winding round the plain, and touching the city at various points, was there let off into the sea. From above, likewise, straight canals of a hundred feet in width were cut in the plain, and again let off into the ditch, toward the sea; these canals were at intervals of a Hundred stadia, and by them they brought, down the wood from the mountains to the city, and conveyed the fruits of the earth in ships, cutting transverse passages from one canal into another, and to the city. Twice in the year they gathered the fruits of the earth--in winter having the benefit of the rains, and in summer introducing the water of the canals. As to the population, each of the lots in the plain had an appointed chief of men who were fit for military service, and the size of the lot was to be a square of ten stadia each way, and the total number of all the lots was sixty thousand.

"And of the inhabitants of the mountains and of the rest of the country there was also a vast multitude having leaders, to whom they were assigned according to their dwellings and villages. The leader was required to furnish for the war the sixth portion of a war-chariot, so as to make up a total of ten thousand chariots; also two horses and riders upon them, and a light chariot without a seat, accompanied by a fighting man on foot carrying a small shield, and having a charioteer mounted to guide the horses; also, be was bound to furnish two heavy-armed men, two archers, two slingers, three stone-shooters, and three javelin men, who were skirmishers, and four sailors to make up a complement of twelve hundred ships. Such was the order of war in the royal city--that of the other nine governments was different in each of them, and would be wearisome to narrate. As to offices and honours, the following was the arrangement from the first: Each of the ten kings, in his own division and in his own city, had the absolute control of the citizens, and in many cases of the laws, punishing and slaying whomsoever be would.

"Now the relations of their governments to one another were regulated by the injunctions of Poseidon as the law had handed them down. These were inscribed by the first men on a column of orichalcum, which was situated in the middle of the island, at the temple of Poseidon, whither the people were gathered together every fifth and sixth years alternately, thus giving equal honor to the odd and to the even number. And when they were gathered together they consulted about public affairs, and inquired if anyone had transgressed in anything, and passed judgment on him accordingly--and before they passed judgment they gave their pledges to one another in this wise: There were bulls who had the range of the temple of Poseidon; and the ten who were left alone in the temple, after they had offered prayers to the gods that they might take the sacrifices which were acceptable to them, hunted the bulls without weapons, but with staves and nooses; and the bull which they caught they led up to the column; the victim was then struck on the head by them, and slain over the sacred inscription, Now on the column, besides the law, there was inscribed an oath invoking mighty curses on the disobedient. When, therefore, after offering sacrifice according to their customs, they had burnt the limbs of the bull, they mingled a cup and cast in a clot of blood for each of them; the rest of the victim they took to the fire, after having made a purification of the column all round. Then they drew from the cup in golden vessels, and, pouring a libation on the fire, they swore that they would judge according to the laws on the column, and would punish anyone who had previously transgressed, and that for the future they would not, if they could help, transgress any of the inscriptions, and would not command or obey any ruler who commanded them to act otherwise than according to the laws of their father Poseidon. This was the prayer which each of them offered up for himself and for his family, at the same time drinking, and dedicating the vessel in the temple of the god; and, after spending some necessary time at supper, when darkness came on and the fire about the sacrifice was cool, all of them put on most beautiful azure robes, and, sitting on the ground at night near the embers of the sacrifices on which they had sworn, and extinguishing all the fire about the temple, they received and gave judgement, if any of them had any accusation to bring against any one; and, when they had given judgment, at daybreak they wrote down their sentences on a golden tablet, and deposited them as memorials with their robes. There were many special laws which the several kings had inscribed about the temples, but the most important was the following: That they were not to take up arms against one another, and they were all to come to the rescue if anyone in any city attempted to over. throw the royal house. Like their ancestors, they were to deliberate in common about war and other matters, giving the supremacy to the family of Atlas; and the king was not to have the power of life and death over any of his kinsmen, unless he had the assent of the majority of the ten kings.

"Such was the vast power which the god settled in the lost island of Atlantis; and this he afterward directed against our land on the following pretext, as traditions tell: For many generations, as long as the divine nature lasted in them, they were obedient to the laws, and well-affectioned toward the gods, who were their kinsmen; for they possessed true and in every way great spirits, practising gentleness and wisdom in the various chances of life, and in their intercourse with one another. They despised everything but virtue, not caring for their present state of life, arid thinking lightly on the possession of gold and other property, which seemed only a burden to them; neither were they intoxicated by luxury; nor did wealth deprive them of their self-control; but they were sober, and saw clearly that all these goods are increased by virtuous friendship with one another, and that by excessive zeal for them, and honor of them, the good of them is lost, and friendship perishes with them.

"By such reflections, and by the continuance in them of a divine nature, all that which we have described waxed and increased in them; but when this divine portion began to fade away in them, and became diluted too often, and with too much of the mortal admixture, and the human nature got the upper-hand, then, they being unable to bear their fortune, became unseemly, and to him who had an eye to see, they began to appear base, and had lost the fairest of their precious gifts; but to those who had no eye to see the true happiness, they still appeared glorious and blessed at the very time when they were filled with unrighteous avarice and power. Zeus, the god of gods, who rules with law, and is able to see into such things, perceiving that an honourable race was in a most wretched state, and wanting to inflict punishment on them, that they might be chastened and improved, collected all the gods into his most holy habitation, which, being placed in the centre of the world, sees all things that partake of generation. And when he had called them together he spake as follows:"

[Here Plato's story abruptly ends.]

Bibliography

Apollodorus (2nd cent bc) *The Library* with English Trans. By Robin Hard, Oxford University Press, Oxford 1977

Apollonius of Rhodes (c.3rd cent bc) *Argonautica* with English trans. By R.V.Rieu, Penguin Classics, London 1971

Avienus, Rufus Festus (4th cent ad) *Ora Maritima* Edited by J.P.Murphy, Ares Publishers, Chicago 1977

Banhoff, Arthur *The early and middle Bronze-age of South Eastern Europe* Charles Scriber & Sons, London 2004

Barber Elizabeth Wayland , *The Mummies of Urumchi* , Macmillan ,London 1999

Briard, Jaques *The Bronze Age in Europe* with English Trans. By Mary Turton , Routledge & Keegan Paul Ltd., London 1979

Bullfinch, Thomas *The Golden Age of Myth and Legend* , Senate, London 1984

Burl, Aubrey *The Stone Circles of Britain and Ireland* , Yale University Press, New Haven and London 2000

Caesar, Julius (100-44bc) *The Conquest of Gaul* with English Trans. By S.A.Handford, Penguin Classics, London 1951

Casson, Lionel *Ships and Seafaring in ancient times*, British Museum, London 1994

Chadwick, John *The Decipherment of Linear B*, University Press, Cambridge 1990

Childe, V.Gordon *Prehistoric communities of British isles*, Chambers,Edinburgh 1956

Cline, Eric H *Plate tectonics and earthquake storms in the late Bronze age Aegean* etc. Journal Archaeological Sci 27 (2000) p47-63

Coles, Bryony and John *Sweet Track to Glastonbury* , Thames and Hudson, London 1986

Conti, Ama et al , *Geochemistry of the formation waters in the Po plain* Applied Geochemistry 15 (2000) 51-65

Cotterell, Arthur *The Minoan World* , Lowe and Brydone Ltd., Thetford 1979

Cremaschi , Mauro et al *Water Management and land use in Terramare* Quaternary Intl 151, 87-98 2006

Cunliffe, Barry *The Oxford Illustrated Prehistory of Europe*, Oxford University Press, Oxford 1994

Demakopoulou et al., *Gods and Heroes of the European Bronze Age*, Thames and Hudson 1999

Diodoris Siculus (60-30bc) *Bibliothica Historica* with English Trans, Loeb Classical Library, London

Donelly, Ignatius *Atlantis, the antedeluvian world*, Gramercy Publishing Co. NY, New York 1985

Drews, Robert *The end of the Bronze Age* , Princeton University Press , NJ 1993

Emanuel, Jeffrey P *Examining Odysseus' raid on Egypt in the late bronze age,* Centre for Hellenistic studies, Harvard

Euripides (c.484-406bc) *Cyclops* with English Trans. By Heather McHugh, Oxford University Press 2001

Euripides (c.484-406bc) *Hippolytus* with English Trans. Oxford University Press 2001

Eusebius of Caesarea (250-341ad) *Chronicon*

Fell, Barry *Bronze Age America* , Little Brown & Co., Boston 1982

Gimbutas, Marija *The Goddesses and Gods of Old Europe* , Thames and Hudson, London 1992

Glob, P.V. *The Mound People* with English trans by Joan Bulman, Book Club Assoc., London 1973

Gurney, O.R. *The Hittites* , Penguin, London 1990

Harbison , Peter *Pre-Christian Ireland* Thames and Hudson, London 1998

Harding,A.F., *European Societies in the Bronze Age*, Cambridge University Press, Cambridge 2000

Herodotus (c484-420bc) *The Histories* with English Trans. By A.R.Burn, Penguin Classics, London

Hesiod (c750bc) *Theogony-Works and Days* with English Trans. By M.L.West, Oxford University Press 1988

Homer (8th cent bc?) *The Iliad* with English Trans by E.V.Rieu, Penguin Classics, London 1950

Homer (8th cent bc?) *The Odyssey* with English Trans by E.V.Rieu, Penguin Classics, London 1946

Karageorgis , Vassos *The Ancient civilisation of Cyprus,* Cowles Educational Corp., New York 1969

Kendrick ,T.D. *The Druids* , Guernsey Press, Guernsey 1996

Kramer ,Samuel Noah *Mythologies of the ancient world* Anchor Books, New York 1961

Kristian Kristiansen and Thomas B.Larsson *The Rise of Bronze Age Society* , University Press, Cambridge 2005

Lamb, H.H. *Climate History and the Modern World* , Methuen, London 1982

Lytton, Lord *Athens its rise and fall* Routledge , London 1874

MacQueen J.G. *The Hittites*, Thames and Hudson, London 1986

Mallory, J.P. *In Search of the Indo Europeans* , Thames and Hudson 1994

Massimo, Fabris et al *Estimation of subsidence in Po delta area* Intl Journal of Geoscience 2014 p51-585

Mazatico, Franco and Tecciato Umberto *The Bronze Age in Trentino and Alto Adige* Prestoria Alpina v34 (1998) p27-60

Menotti, Francesco *Living on the lake in prehistoric Europe* Routledge , London 2004

Pausanias (c110-180ad) *Guide to Greece* with English trans. By R.V.Rieu, Penguin Classics, London 1971

Piovan , Siovan *Bronze-age paleohydrography of the Southern Venetian plain Geoarchaeology* vol25 N1 6-35 (2010)

Piovan, Siovan and Mozzi, Paolo *Recognising avulsion events in the Adige river alluvial system* Ital.Jou. of Quat. Sci. 24 p120-122

Plato (c.427-347bc) *Timaeus and Critias* with English Trans by Desmond Lee. Penguin Classics, London 1977

Pliny (Gaius Plinius Secundus 23-29ad) *Natural History* with English Trans, Loeb Classical Library, London

Poulet, Gabrielle et al *Bronze Age Pottery from Verona*

Singerland, Rudy and Smith, Norman D *River avulsions and their deposits* Ann Rev Earth Planet Science 2004 32 p257-281

Spanuth J, *Atlantis of the North* , Sidgwick and Jackson, London 1979

Spanuth.J *Atlantis the Mystery Unravelled* , Arco Publishers, London 1956

Spindler, Konrad *The Man in the Ice* , Wiedenfield and Nicholson, London 1994

St Jerome, *The Chronicon* (347-420)

Starr , Chester G *The Origins of Greek Civilisation* , Norton & Co., London 1961

Strabo (c.64bc-24ad) *Geographica* with English Trans, Loeb Classical Library, London

Whitehouse, Ruth *Investigating surface archaeology on the Po flood plain* Archaeology Intl

Index

15933687R00104

Printed in Great Britain
by Amazon